MO'S BOWS

A YOUNG PERSON'S
GUIDE TO START-UP SUCCESS

MEASURE, CUT, STITCH YOUR WAY
TO A GREAT BUSINESS

BY
MOZIAH BRIDGES
WITH TRAMICA MORRIS
FOREWORD BY DAYMOND JOHN

RP|KIDS
PHILADELPHIA

The image on page vi is courtesy of Audria Richmond.
The images on pages x, 13, 40, 63, 71, 78–79, 87, 101, 149, and 160
are courtesy of Annabella Charles.
The image on page 7 is courtesy of the White House.
The images on pages 8 and 93 are courtesy of Demarcus Bowser.
The images on pages 19, 22, 31, and 95 are courtesy of Tramica Morris.
The image on page 58 is courtesy of Steven Palmer.
The image on page 117 is courtesy of Lindsey Lissau.
The image on pages 140–141 is courtesy of Commercial Appeal.

Running Press Kids
Hachette Book Group
1290 Avenue of the Americas, New York, NY 10104
www.runningpress.com/rpkids
@RP_Kids

Printed in the United States of America

First Edition: October 2019

Published by Running Press Kids, an imprint of Perseus Books, LLC,
a subsidiary of Hachette Book Group, Inc. The Running Press Kids name
and logo is a trademark of the Hachette Book Group.

The Hachette Speakers Bureau provides a wide range of authors for speaking
events. To find out more, go to www.hachettespeakersbureau.com
or call (866) 376-6591.

The publisher is not responsible for websites (or their content)
that are not owned by the publisher.

Print book cover and interior design by Frances J. Soo Ping Chow.

Library of Congress Control Number: 2018948410

ISBNs: 978-0-7624-9251-0 (paperback), 978-0-7624-9250-3 (ebook)

LSC-C

10 9 8 7 6 5 4 3 2 1

❖

Dedicated to my parents,

Tramica Morris and Clete Bridges,

who have gifted me with my creative style

and entrepreneurial spirit.

Also, to Granny Galloway, Granny Cleasant,

my aunts, uncles, cousins, brother, and sister:

thanks for keeping me grounded.

In loving memory of

Granny Gladys and Sonia Faylene Bryant,

who always reminded me to shine bright

like the star that I am.

❖

CONTENTS

FOREWORD
BY DAYMOND JOHN

The first time I met Mo Bridges, he was eleven years old. It was 2013, and from the second he walked onto *Shark Tank* to pitch his company, Mo's Bows, I knew Mo was unique. Mo was smart and well spoken; I could tell he had a purpose. Even at eleven, he understood his business better than adults who have pitched me for years. (Just don't let them know that.) I saw the passion he had for his work and was impressed by his commitment. In the Tank, Mo was offered a deal by none other than Kevin O'Leary, a.k.a. Mr. Wonderful (and for anyone who has seen the show, you know Kevin's offers aren't always wonderful). I advised Mo not to take the deal. I could see he was on the brink of growing Mo's Bows into something huge. If he accepted the money from Kevin, he'd also have to pay him a royalty from every bow tie sold (typical O'Leary offer!). I wanted to help Mo grow his business in a way that kept him in control of the company and its profits. I wanted to offer him guidance I didn't have when I was starting out. As I told him right then on *Shark Tank*: the mentoring I could offer was more valuable than just taking the money.

Mo reminds me of myself in many ways, with his innovation, his determination, and, gotta say it, his style. But I'm most impressed by Mo's hustle. He got himself on *Shark Tank* at a young age and didn't let surprises stop him from achieving his dream. Mo's success proves that you can find the resources to start a company at any age, even as a kid. You just have to know where to look. For Mo, that meant reaching out to his mom and grandmother. His mom helped promote Mo's Bows on Facebook and drove Mo to trunk shows in the early days of his business. His grandmother helped him make his first two thousand ties by hand, right in their kitchen. Making it a family effort didn't make it any less Mo's business. Asking for help when he needed it—and, better still, recognizing a smart collaboration when it was in front of him—was another necessary step.

It takes time for most to realize there's more to building a business than being a friendly person or a sharp dresser. You need the drive to succeed. I always say that entrepreneurs aren't visionaries, but at the same time they don't hesitate to do whatever it takes to make their idea a reality. That is exactly what Mo did, and today he is running his own company. Being an entrepreneur isn't like any other job because you're never really "done." The moment you complete a project, it's on to the next thing. Great CEOs can think about multiple steps at the same time. The best CEOs are always growing, always finding new ways to create and reach new consumers. That's why when you're young, it's important to get yourself moving early.

Even today, I see more of myself in Mo. He's hardworking, he's dedicated, and he loves the work that he does. His success is no accident. Young entrepreneurs can learn from Mo's experiences, and I'm pleased to say that I have as well. He's an inspiration for the next generation of creators—a true force for change. Mo sets goals for himself that he finds ways to exceed. I can't think of any other entrepreneur his age that has been honored by the White House, has deals in place with the National Basketball Association (NBA), and whose book is in your hands right now. From his earliest days in business, Mo understood his customers, and he continues inventing ways to keep them coming back to Mo's Bows. He has a knack for **sales**, and plenty of flair, and he has the product to back it up.

Listen to Mo's story. Learn his experiences. If you're an aspiring entrepreneur, don't let your age make you feel like your dreams are out of reach. As you're about to read, Mo was lucky to find success at a young age, but he worked hard for it, too. It's never too early to find confidence in yourself and to start building your empire. Start out early like Mo did, and soon you'll develop your own strategies for success.

I'm honored I've had the opportunity to mentor such a bright, skilled, and creative young man, and I can't wait to see what Mo does next.

Daymond John

New York City

2018

HANDCRAFTED

MO'S BOWS

BOW TIES

EST. 2011

A YOUNG PERSON'S GUIDE
TO START-UP SUCCESS

1

START TODAY!

ENTREPRENEURSHIP IS THE PURSUIT OF OPPORTUNITY WITHOUT REGARD TO RESOURCES CURRENTLY CONTROLLED.

**—PROFESSOR HOWARD STEVENSON,
HARVARD BUSINESS SCHOOL**

Hello there, young **entrepreneur**! I'm going to call you that a lot because that's how I see you, and soon you will see yourself as that, too. What I need to tell you right now will change your future and put you on a path that everyone wants but few are willing to work for. We all come from different places and different backgrounds. But if you look at successful inventors and entrepreneurs, what's the only thing they have in common? They were all kids once, just like us. And they all had a dream, just like we do.

Do you have an idea for a business, an app, or a **service**? Are you always thinking of inventions that you wish were in the world already? Then this book will hopefully help you by being a step-by-step guide on how to turn those dreams into reality.

I am fired up and ready to share with you the secrets of business that took me a long time to learn. In fact, this is the book that I wish I had read before I became an entrepreneur. When I started my company, Mo's Bows, in 2011, there were no real resources for young entrepreneurs on the market, and it seemed like every time I thought I got somewhere, I had to start all over. But lucky for you, we have each other. And I'm here to help give you the tools you need to start *your* business and to help it thrive.

Maybe you're asking yourself, *Why should I listen to some kid? Who is this guy anyway to give me advice?* Let me give you a little bit of backstory, so you know more about who I am and what advice I have to offer you.

Eight years ago I started a small bow tie business—Mo's Bows—with the help of my mom and granny. One day I was out trying to sell my product, one bow tie at a time, and suddenly the next day I found myself sending hundreds of bow ties to places like Neiman Marcus, Bloomingdale's, Cole Haan, and the Home Shopping Network. Today, I continue to partner with major companies that believe in my work and vision (organizations like the NBA and St. Jude's Children's Hospital, to name two).

Between being a creative director, acting as the face of my own fashion brand, and traveling around the world meeting new

people, I've learned so many skills that have made me a successful kidpreneur—skills like great communication, creativity, and
having the desire to help others by giving back to the community.
The lessons I learned early in my career were so powerful that
even at eleven years old, I blew away some of the biggest names in
business when I appeared on the hit ABC TV show *Shark Tank*. I
have grown and learned even more since then, and I can't wait to
tell you all about it so that when you are on *Shark Tank* someday,
pitching your business to a panel of successful businesspeople,
you will be even better prepared than I was.

Long before *Shark Tank*, though, Mo's Bows did have a small
customer base that followed me on social media. And people
started contacting me with orders from all over the world as they
heard about what I had to offer through the Internet and by word
of mouth. Over the years, business writers have also featured Mo's
Bows in the *New York Times, Forbes,* and *O: The Oprah Magazine.*

Writers and interviewers always asked me a similar question
when I first started Mo's Bows: "What's the secret? What do you
know at ten that most adults haven't even figured out?"

The short answer is that everything you need in order to succeed already exists inside you. Your talent, your passion, and your
determination are the biggest keys to your success.

The long answer is everything we will talk about in this book.
These are the tools you can use in order to succeed.

I want to share with you my business secrets because I know
that success breeds success. People will tell you that you're just
a kid and that starting a business is super hard. But I'm also a
kid. And when I started my business, I could never have dreamed
of where I would be today. If I could go back in time and tell my
younger self all the bright things in my future, even little Mo

wouldn't believe it (after he got over the whole time-travel thing, of course). He would probably fall over in shock hearing future Mo say, "A year from today some of your ties will be on display in the Tennessee State Museum, but you'll be too busy getting to work the red carpet as a fashion correspondent for the NBA Draft to fully appreciate it."

Unfortunately, I don't have a time machine (yet). But if that changes, I would absolutely go back in time and give myself this book. That's because I used the secrets I have outlined here, and I was able to start from nothing, turning a small idea for a bow tie business into an international brand with a very loyal Instagram following as well. I've had the chance to travel to the White House and meet President Barack Obama, giving him a special satin royal-blue bow tie called the "Obama Blue Bow Tie." I've gotten to go on several TV shows, like *The Steve Harvey Show*, *Wonderama*, and *Good Morning America*. I was also featured in *O: The Oprah Magazine* and was twice on *Time*'s list of "30 Most Influential Teens." Last year I was asked to share my story onstage in front of more than five thousand people at the CUNA Government Affairs Conference. That was my biggest crowd so far, and after leaving the stage I was even able to meet and talk with former president George W. Bush, who was speaking after me.

These days, I travel around the world selling bow ties and sharing my story with young and old entrepreneurs—and with parents and children. I like to share my story and encourage others—especially young people—to dream big and not to wait until they get older to figure out what they want to do. As a young person, you have to strike while the iron is hot, and so if creating your own business is what you want to do now, I say, "Start today!"

Whether you're fifteen or fifty-five, you can pick up this book today and start building the future that you want for yourself. Yes, I mean you! You can have an exhibit dedicated to you in your home state or see your face in magazines, even though you have no formal training in business.

In the following pages, I'm going to show you how to pursue your dreams and to reach your goals in business. It's my promise to you—kid to kid.

HOW TO USE THIS BOOK

The hardest part in business is figuring out how to take a good idea you have and make it even better. Through a lot of trial and error, I have come up with a system that will help you start with nothing and chase your dreams, making them a reality. I call my system Measure—Cut—Stitch. Whether you're making a bow tie or creating a new app, you can learn the process right away, but only if you measure out what you need, cut it into parts, and then stitch it together. For that reason, this book is divided into three parts to help explain how to get your business up and running: "Measure," "Cut," and "Stitch."

To begin, in "Measure" I'm going to tell you a little bit about how I first got started with my business. I will show you how I was able to get my business going from zero dollars to making a profit. In this first part you will find ways to get hold of the resources you need to get your business ideas out of your head and into the hands of your first customers.

Being able to spot opportunities for your business will make your career as an entrepreneur flourish from day one. The advice and tips I provide in "Measure" will tell you how to get your business off the ground starting today by helping you find *free* resources. Anybody anywhere, with little or no money, can start a business, take stock in what resources they have available, and start building upon existing dreams. You just need to measure out your goals or reasons for wanting to start a business. I'll also help you to measure the time it will take you to meet your goals and to also assess what you want your life to look like once you have succeeded in starting your very own business.

"Cut" is the next part, and in it I will help you to get your business in motion. Making decisions and planning ahead and then evaluating the success of what you are doing are all an important part of this process. This section will help you to break down what kind of business you want to start based on the things you like or are passionate about.

Finally, "Stitch" offers tips and advice on how to put everything together. I'm going to show you everything I know and how I learned it. And in the end, you are going to put it all together so you can get your first **venture** off the ground.

When I started Mo's Bows, I didn't really have the tools that I now use to run my business. Even worse, I thought I could never get started unless I had everything in place at the very start. A lot of people have an idea for a business or an app or a service, but they never see it realized because they don't know where to start. Every business needs tools to get going; just as a builder uses tools to construct a house, you will need tools to build your business. So I'm going to give you a tool for free right now.

All you have to do is remember the following: Mo's **BOWS of Business**.

Whatever challenge you're facing today—in school, life, or business—you can improve your position by checking in with the following BOWS:

BELIEVE in yourself

OPPORTUNITIES—find ways to give back

WORK HARD

SUPPORT from friends and family

We'll come back to Mo's BOWS of Business again and again throughout the book, so don't worry about remembering them right now. You'll be an expert by book's end.

So, without any more delay, let's get going!

M E A S U R E

To start off we are going to measure what we're working with.
This is something I do all the time as a designer, but it's actually something that is even more important to me as an entrepreneur. In fashion and manufacturing, people have a saying: "Measure once, cut twice." But entrepreneurs are always measuring: What are our resources? What is the demand in the market? Where could we improve?

Later we will make some cuts and stitch them together. But for now let's talk about how to get started by measuring.

2

BUILD WHAT YOU WANT TO SEE IN THE WORLD!

I remember my dad and granddad wearing bow ties when I was a young boy. I noticed that they would wear really nice suits and bow ties for no special occasion. So whenever my parents allowed me to dress myself, I would put on a suit and a necktie—I thought it was a pretty normal thing to do. I'd even wear a suit and tie to the playground! I also remember seeing Jay-Z and Justin Timberlake on an awards show once, and they were wearing bow ties. And I thought, *With the right tie, you can look like you've already won an award.*

The problem was, I couldn't find anybody making cool and edgy bow ties for kids. I could sometimes find kids' bow ties made from cheap nylon material or clip-on ties that looked silly and wacky. I was very young, but it didn't take me long to figure out that men generally tie their own bow ties and that clip-ons were not for me. While shopping in department stores, I would always look for a bow tie or necktie print that spoke to me; I wanted my clothes to energize me when I wore them. But I simply could not find those kind of cool bow ties. The self-tie bow ties that I did finally find were simply too expensive and only came in adult sizes from top designers. Plus, at seven years old, let's face it, my mom was not likely to spend fifty dollars on a bow tie for me when I might easily get mustard or my favorite chocolate candy on it.

Two years later, when I turned nine, I finally took action. At the time I wasn't thinking about starting a business or even getting into fashion. I just knew I wanted to wear a fun bow tie that represented me and my style. I couldn't be the only kid on earth who wanted to look cool like Jay-Z and Justin Timberlake, could I? I knew I wanted to create a special bow tie just for me, and I started to wonder if I could make that dream a reality.

When I finally tried, I gotta tell you—it didn't go so well.

"No, no, no!" I screamed when the sewing machine ate my first attempt at creating a bow tie. The stitching just ran away from me. After weeks of trying to find the perfect bow tie, I went over to my granny's house, and she promised to show me how to make my own bow tie out of vintage material scraps.

At the time, my mom was working full-time, so I'd often hang out with my granny after school until Mom got off work. We spent a lot of time together that year. But the hard thing for my granny is that she had a stroke when I was younger. She isn't able to move the whole right side of her body, and she has to do almost every-thing with only one hand. Although it is difficult for her to move around quickly, she is still a fun and vibrant granny. She doesn't like to fuss with her hair, so, even though she doesn't have to, she wears a short gray wig. She walks with a cane and always keeps it by her when she's on the couch or at the dinner table so she doesn't have to depend on anyone else to help her get around.

For more than fifty years, Granny worked as a seamstress, and over the years she kept scraps of fabric that other people would just throw away. I knew if anyone could help me create my perfect bow tie, it would be my granny.

I had this idea in my head of the perfect bow tie—nice "wings" coming out the side, a cool color, and stitching on both sides that would be perfectly even. So even, in fact, that people would be surprised that the bow tie was a self-tie bow tie.

But my dream was going downhill as the sewing machine mangled my bow tie.

"One step at a time, sweetie," Granny told a hysterical me, as she pulled the bow tie fabric out of the sewing machine. Not only did the thread get stuck in the fabric, but now the machine needed to be rethreaded from all the knots I'd created. My mom always gave me grief when I broke something, so I would absolutely die if I destroyed my granny's sewing machine.

I examined the mangled tie after Granny got it unstuck. And when I say this tie looked messed up, I mean it. The stitching was all ragged and uneven. The two sides of the bow tie were different sizes. I couldn't even tie it if I wanted to because one side had come undone. And the worst part was that I had stitched the tie shut. Instead of a nice, fluffy bow in the middle, the fabric dipped inward. It was completely ruined.

I sat there, wondering how anyone could actually make their own clothes. My fashion dreams were crumbling in that moment. I felt like crying but didn't want to in front of Granny.

"I'm never gonna get this, Granny!" I remember saying, completely exasperated.

As I sat there, feeling sorry for myself, I noticed how patient Granny was. She couldn't grab anything with her right hand and really needed two hands to run the sewing machine. But she carefully lifted her right hand with her left and placed it on top of the bow tie. Then with her good left hand she flattened out the fabric and reversed the machine to pull it free. It took her extra time to do all of this, but she didn't give up.

She told me to be patient as she lifted her good hand and grabbed a pointed tool called a seam ripper. "Watch this," she said.

I didn't know how she did it, but she pulled loose one thread, and then all the stitches just came out—*zip zip zip*. It was like pulling out a shoelace. That one tiny thread came undone like it was nothing.

"Easily done, easily undone. This will be your best friend while you're learning," she said and handed me the seam ripper, handle first.

Granny laid out the fabric and placed it back on the ironing board. With just two puffs of steam it looked brand-new. I couldn't even see all the little holes from where the needle had pierced through with my messed-up stitch.

Two minutes later, Granny pulled that first bow tie out of the machine. And that's when I realized that even though I wasn't great at sewing, I just needed to be patient like my granny and eventually I would learn to make bow ties with my own two hands.

I tied the bow tie around my neck and looked in the mirror. In that moment, I knew that my life was going to change. That bow tie made me feel like I was wearing a nice big smile on my collar.

I still have my first bow tie. I know now where I could have

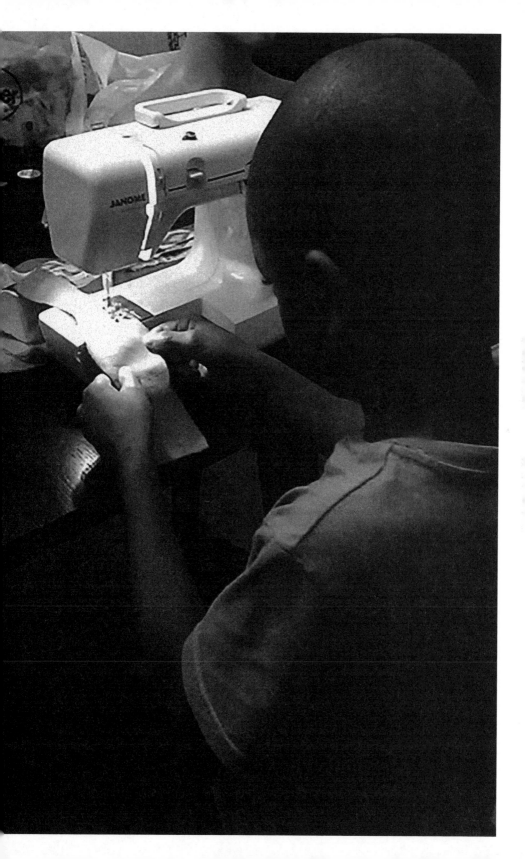

sewn straighter; I know that the scrap of fabric was old and faded and that it doesn't go with anything I'd want to be seen wearing today. But I'll never forget the way Granny looked at me that day in the mirror, like I could do anything I set my mind to.

Now, I bet a lot of you secretly want to be entrepreneurs and that's why you've picked up this book. You'd love to design a cool new app or video game or start a business of your own. But a lot of people are afraid of what others will think of them and their dreams. When I first thought about making my own bow ties, I would ask myself things like, *What if becoming an entrepreneur turns your friends into haters? What if people see me fail? What if people don't take me serious as a young businessman? What if no one likes my awesome bow ties?*

I decided quickly that I wouldn't worry about any of that. In any start-up business, you want to focus first on making your **MVP**, your **minimum viable product**, the simplest form of what you are trying to offer to the public. Was my first bow tie perfect? No. But I didn't spend any time worrying about that. Instead, the day after making it, I wore my first bow tie to school.

I believe that when you look good, you feel good. And when I wore my handmade bow tie to school, I could tell the other kids thought I had something special.

That day I wore my bow tie to school with pride. Maybe I was the only kid in the world who wanted to wear a nice bow tie. I didn't think then that I had a major fashion brand on my hands. But I did ask Granny if we could make some more bow ties because kids in my class were starting to ask me for them.

First, kids would trade me some chips from their lunch if I gave them one of my bow ties. Soon, I could trade a bow tie for candy or even these cool crystal rocks that the other boys had.

You'd think elementary school–age boys wouldn't have many places to wear a bow tie and wouldn't really want one in the first place. (I mean, we're not all winning an Oscar every day.) I was worried that my teacher would put a stop to my business plans. But she could tell that I was learning an important skill, and she wanted to support it. So she decided we should start Bow Tie Wednesdays. And these special Wednesdays soon created even more demand for my bow ties from my classmates, who now had a way to showcase their new bow tie each week.

Looking back, if I had started with just focusing on how to make money by selling bow ties, I wouldn't have made a dime. My mom would see me come home and be shocked that I had no tie because I sold it for valueless items. She thought that it was so crazy, but as a businessman I had to do what I had to do. Instead, I let my passion for fashion drive my business, and the demand simply came to me. By offering other kids the chance to look and feel good, the interest in my bow ties grew. Soon, I had to start producing more on a weekly basis.

It made me feel good to see so many people wearing my bow ties. In fact, I would not have minded just making free bow ties out of my granny's scrap fabric forever. But when a friend asked for a custom white bow tie, I knew I had to charge him something for it because my granny didn't have white fabric in her stash and that meant I'd now have to spend money to buy special fabric just to create this one tie.

I didn't charge my friend much for the bow tie—just five dollars—but after that, I started making ties with nice fabric,

charging five dollars per bow tie at first and then eventually raising the price to fifteen dollars once I realized that I made nicer bow ties than anything people could find in the store. A lot of other kids wanted to look good and feel good in my product, it seemed, and that made me realize I could start making a profit out of this demand.

Starting your own business and running it successfully can be overwhelming, but if you can remember why you're passionate about what you're doing, it doesn't feel like work!

It's time to check in with the BOWS of Business. At the time I started my business, I didn't know a single thing about fashion or sewing, but I did:

BELIEVE in myself! That first bow tie could have been my last. But I decided to go back and try again.

Find OPPORTUNITIES to give back. I knew other kids probably couldn't find or afford bow ties that they liked just as I did. Plus, every day I kept sewing, I learned how to make the ties better. So I gave them away for free for a while.

WORK HARD. My original goal was just to have one bow tie to wear. But I worked harder to make more and better ties.

Have SUPPORT from friends and family. This was a double whammy. My granny had so much scrap fabric and the time to teach me how to sew so I could get better at making my product. And my friends at school were my first models, customers, and supporters!

As you get ready to jump into the next chapter, think about what BOWS you already have in your life that will help you on your way to starting your business.

CHAPTER

3

MAKE SUCCESS A PART OF EVERY DAY!

As an entrepreneur, you learn to see the world differently. You might get an allowance for doing your chores. Or you may have a job after school that doesn't pay very well. Babysitting or mowing lawns might be great for making a small amount of money today, but as an entrepreneur, you will put in the work now to create better opportunities for yourself later in life.

Here is an example of how an entrepreneur might see a situation differently: Imagine that an employee makes $8 an hour mowing lawns for a landscaper. At the end of a five-hour day, he makes $40. A young entrepreneur hears about this and decides to find five lawns to mow for $20 each. She then brings in $100 on a single Saturday afternoon.

Reading the example above, a part of you may wonder, *Could I do that?*

I'm here to tell you yes, you absolutely could do that if you put your mind to it and work hard.

I'm going to let you in on a few secrets about entrepreneurs to help you become a successful one:

1. Entrepreneurs are everywhere! You don't have to be designing an app in a secret hideout to be considered an entrepreneur. The skills of an entrepreneur are valuable to anybody at any level of business—whether you're just getting started or already working for someone else.

2. Entrepreneurship takes practice! Whether you are opening a lemonade stand or a lawn-mowing business, your *real* business is building the business that can handle *more* business. In the example of the lawn mower making $40 a day, if he spent just one day planning out how to find new customers, he could start earning $20 extra each day for doing just *one* more lawn. But success doesn't come easy at all; it comes with hard work and determination.

3. Entrepreneurs need to be entrepreneurs of every task in front of them. You will become like a mad scientist, always tweaking and testing out new ways of working and becoming more successful.

4. Remember to Measure—Cut—Stitch. Your job is to find your work, plan it out, put it together, and then start over. Once you've mowed your first lawn or sold your first glass of lemonade, you need to ask yourself: *How would I do it differently if I could start over now, knowing what I learned*

today? To do that, you need to measure how the business venture turned out, cut out anything that didn't work, and then stitch it back together.

5. Always have honest accounting. This is the hardest, but most exciting, part of being an entrepreneur. Some people call this the boring stuff, but account management is where you will find what was wasted and how you can make your money go further for you.

So, given all of the above, let's check in with your BOWS of Business and really think about answers to the following questions before you move on to the next chapter:

How can you BELIEVE in yourself?

What are your OPPORTUNITIES to give back?

To get there, how can you WORK HARD?

Who can you count on when you need to SEEK SUPPORT from friends and family?

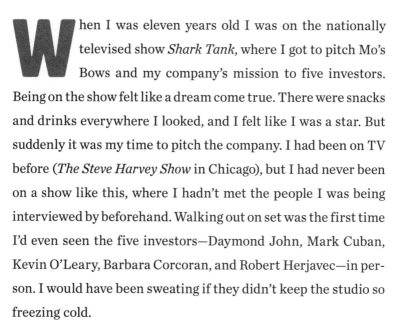

CHAPTER

4

FIGURE OUT YOUR *SHARK TANK* PITCH

When I was eleven years old I was on the nationally televised show *Shark Tank*, where I got to pitch Mo's Bows and my company's mission to five investors. Being on the show felt like a dream come true. There were snacks and drinks everywhere I looked, and I felt like I was a star. But suddenly it was my time to pitch the company. I had been on TV before (*The Steve Harvey Show* in Chicago), but I had never been on a show like this, where I hadn't met the people I was being interviewed by beforehand. Walking out on set was the first time I'd even seen the five investors—Daymond John, Mark Cuban, Kevin O'Leary, Barbara Corcoran, and Robert Herjavec—in person. I would have been sweating if they didn't keep the studio so freezing cold.

People of all ages dream of going on *Shark Tank*. But many appear to think that they can just rattle off some crazy business idea and get Mark Cuban's money and never have to work again. I knew that wasn't the case, however, because I had been hustling my bow ties for two years before I landed on the show. I knew I had to go out there and really convince the Sharks that my business was worth their investment.

I had told the story of my company a hundred times to people—interviewers, producers, and potential customers—but as I approached the Sharks onstage, I found that I just couldn't spit out the words I'd said so many times before.

Every *Shark Tank* pitch is supposed to start the same way. Before going on the show, I received an email from the producers informing me that "all pitches must begin with this format: 'My name is [blank]. My company is [blank]. I'm seeking [blank] in exchange for [blank] percent of my company.'"

I knew that I had started off right because I spoke first, even before my mom did, saying, "My name is Moziah Bridges, and I'm the CEO of Mo's Bows Handmade Bow Ties." I then adjusted the yellow-and-white chevron bow tie around my neck and gave them a big smile, saying, "And I brought with me my lovely momager."

That got the whole room to break into a smile. Mom and I then started to tag team the pitch, and it was smooth sailing: "Sharks, I always like to dress nice. Even when I was little, I would wear a suit and tie just to go and play on the playground. But the problem was I couldn't find any bow ties that I liked."

But more important, getting them to smile helped me get my rhythm. I was so focused on *doing my pitch* that I tripped over my own words, and that kept me from letting the Sharks know who I was. Ideas are more important than words. I wanted them to invest in *me*, not in my pitch.

One thing my mom and I worked on was making sure we knew what to say as our last line. So I told the Sharks a bit more about my company and how much we were looking to raise. I wanted them to know that we were really going places, so I ended by saying, "My only question is, Sharks: Who's coming with me?"

Not everyone, of course, has the opportunity to get on a show like *Shark Tank*. But you don't need to be on *Shark Tank* to make your pitch! Let's do an exercise that even the best and biggest names in business struggle with: telling people what you do and what you want. This exercise focuses on who you are and what you can do for others. Sometimes as a business owner you have to quickly share your business motto or product with someone. You will have to find a very short and concise way to explain it. Most people in business call this the "**elevator pitch**." You've got to hook your listener and sell them yourself and your product

FIGURE OUT YOUR *SHARK TANK* PITCH

in just the amount of time it takes you to complete an average elevator ride.

Remember: You are an entrepreneur. So go for the *"Shark Tank* pitch"* in this situation. What is the best way you can hook a serious investor or customer in the shortest amount of time possible (even a time shorter than an elevator ride)?

Your *Shark Tank* pitch should go something like this: "My name is _____. I am the founder of _____. I'm here today to _____." That last blank lets the person you're talking to know how to respond to what you are seeking, so think about exactly what it is you are seeking to gain or get from them.

Here are some quick examples using two different entrepreneurs. One has a lawn-mowing business, and the other has a lemonade stand.

Example 1 pitch: "My name is Karen, and I am the founder of Karen's Lawn Care. I am ten years old, and I live down the street. I'm here today to tell you how great your yard can look with my company's help."

Example 2 pitch: "My name is Dave, and I am the founder of LemonDave, a unique and delicious homemade lemonade. I am here today to give out a free sample of my lemonade."

See how much we learn about Karen and Dave from their short pitches? We can tell they're entrepreneurs, we can tell they aren't like most kids, and we learn both of them are so passionate about what they do that they want to share it with you. Notice how a person could learn more about what they do at no cost?

Rejection keeps most people from even trying. But by giving a no-cost pitch to people, you are doing several very important things. First of all, you are talking about you and your **brand**. This takes practice! Second, you are generating word of mouth in such a way that people care to share what you do with others. Trust me, the market for high-end bow ties is slim, but the number of people who want to hear about a mother-son team who started their own business is much larger.

If you have an idea for a business—any business—make sure you feel comfortable talking about it. To make your *Shark Tank* pitch even easier, think about a few things about your business: Does it have a name you can easily say aloud? Do people understand what you're looking for from them when you solicit their business? These things will lead you toward becoming only more successful and toward attracting great customers and great business.

When do you think your *Shark Tank* pitch will come in handy? Here are a few times when you can use your pitch in real life:

- It's great for when you see an old family friend or neighbor and they ask what you have been up to.
- It can be very handy when your parents introduce you to new people.
- It works great when you meet someone in a similar industry. They might even give you helpful pointers that will lead you to gain new customers.

Try it out for yourself as you start your business. And after you've given your pitch a few times, focus on how to better get on track—or to get back on track if you feel like you've lost your way in your business goals. It's okay to not have this down perfectly right away. Honestly, it's part of the assignment to try and then retry your business pitch. Learn, explore, tear some things apart, and see if you can put them back together even better the next time.

When I got started making bow ties, my main goal was to look and feel good. I didn't have much of an elevator or *Shark Tank* pitch to begin with because the goal was pretty personal. But shortly after I made that first bow tie, I discovered that a lot of other kids and adults wanted my **product**, too. So I had to figure out how to take my passion for making bow ties to the next level—I had to learn to develop my pitch and then to sell my product to my potential customer.

Where I grew up, I didn't have a lot of local leaders or businesspeople to help me out by being my mentor or giving me resources. I had only a few books that I could turn to (and nothing about being a young businessperson, either). I did find inspiration in the book *Reallionaire*—the story of Farrah Gray, who started his business by selling pet rocks and then flipping the profit from that into beginning another business (he eventually became a millionaire by age eighteen).

I also sought out stories from designer Daymond John. I wasn't as interested in the stories of him pulling down a million in sales, but rather I was captivated by the narrative of him and his mother making hats in their garage when he was just starting out in business. I felt inspired; if Daymond could come from nothing and become one of the most successful figures in fashion and television by the age of twenty, what was stopping me from trying to do the same at nine years old?

What I found by reading these stories is that the people who are most successful early on are the people who are most comfortable talking about their business and aren't afraid of putting themselves out there. And that's what you *have* to do in order to become a successful young entrepreneur.

Remember, if you're stuck as you start thinking about your pitch or if you wonder where you'll use your pitch, turn to the BOWS of Business for guidance:

BELIEVE in your ability to improve over time.

OPPORTUNITIES to give back are always a great way to get word out about your business. In the examples of the lawn-mowing business and the lemonade stand, Karen and Dave offered people helpful information about whether they could save money on their lawn care and about a new beverage.

WORK HARD! Your pitch will change over time, and it might also change depending on who you are talking to. Work on that pitch!

SEEK SUPPORT from friends and family whenever you are doubting your goals or your business. Test out your pitch on someone you trust and ask for their honest feedback, so you can make it even better for those times when you really need it to work for you!

CHAPTER

5

DON'T BE AFRAID
OF FAILURE

Y ou may think that for most nine-year-olds—who are too young to babysit or even to mow lawns—the logical "first business" they would start would be a lemonade stand. But as a nine-year-old, I didn't want to sell lemonade; I wanted to sell bow ties. I had no idea *how* I would do it, but I knew I needed to get my bow ties out in the world. Shortly after making my first bow ties for my classmates, I visited our local farmers' market to set up the equivalent of a lemonade stand for my bow ties.

I stayed up all night making a big Mo's Bows sign for the stand. I wanted everyone to see that I was Mo and that I was selling bow ties. I had my **packaging** ready to go, and I had a little vintage red, white, and blue bazooka lunch box to use as my cash box. In hindsight, though, I was so focused on wanting customers to come to my table for the perfect buying experience that I didn't think about the actual display for my ties. I didn't realize how easily the wind would whip my bow ties and my sign off the table and onto the ground. That first farmers' market, I spent more time chasing down my bow ties than selling them.

Sure, I learned a lot about merchandising that day, and I also got a good amount of practice in doing my pitch every time I came back to the booth and set up my display again. I got to give my pitch to different people at least a dozen times. And I sold five ties by the end of the day, which gave me $125 to put back into my business for the next time.

By some measures, that wasn't a successful afternoon. But imagine how far behind I would be if I were too afraid to try?

Fear keeps us from success more than failure does. Remember: It's okay if you're not ready to start beta testing your first product right this second. Make sure that you don't suffer from "paralysis by analysis," though, which is the idea that you think about starting over again and again before you can even start putting yourself and your product out in front of others.

So many of us don't want to put our name on a product until it's perfect. That extends to our branding and packaging. But perfection is the enemy of *good enough*.

I certainly didn't have the perfect setup for my first farmers' market. But by the end of the first day I learned more by actually doing than I could have learned if I'd just set up a table in my secluded backyard for practice. Was I a failure for running such a poorly managed first farmers' market booth? I don't think so. I was there so that other people could look good and feel good, just like me, and now I knew exactly what *not* to do the next time I set up a stand on a windy day.

And you know what the wildest part of this experience is? I went back to that same farmers' market soon after my first showing. I set up my bow ties in a vintage suitcase display this time, so they weren't so easy for the wind to scatter all over the ground. I secured a Mo's Bows Handmade Bow Ties sign to the legs of my tent so it wouldn't blow away. That image turned out to be one of our most iconic symbols—the young man hitting the streets with a suitcase of bow ties to sell. This image showed people everything they needed to know about me, and I wouldn't have figured that out if I'd been too afraid to try.

Here's the truth about goals: setting them matters so much more than achieving them. Your goals for your business will likely change as you learn and adapt to the new things you discover along the way. Keep in mind what you want and why you want it—that's your motivation, and *that's* sometimes the key to being a successful entrepreneur.

What motivates you to start and be in business? Do you just want some extra money? Do you want to save for a new bike or a new life? All the work you do will help you get there. You just have to take a leap and start!

Here's how I was able to work through my goals when I first started my business:

On day 1 I had a simple goal: **Look good and feel good.**

On day 2 that goal changed: **Make a bow tie I like.**

On day 3 I had achieved all my goals, but a friend asked me if I could make him a bow tie, so I set a new goal: **Make bow ties for others.**

On day 4 I started over with what I'd been looking for and couldn't find: **Help others to look good and feel good.**

Every time I achieved a new goal, it felt like reaching a new level in a video game, and after that I was prepared to take on the next level until I reached the game's end. I knew I would make

some mistakes along the way, and after completing a level I also knew that I could do that level even better now with some hindsight. But I had leveled up nonetheless! After finishing a level, it wouldn't make sense for me to keep playing that level over and over again.

So I learned to set new goals—to reach for new levels.

However, all along, through each level, I really had one *major* goal: **Help other people look good and feel good.** And while that goal has shifted and morphed over the years as my business has grown and changed, it's remained important to me to get my business right so that I can continue reaching my main goal.

So ask yourself today: What can you do *right now* to start achieving your first goal? Don't just keep setting higher and higher goals, but really stop and determine how you can achieve your ultimate goal and then set out smaller goals that you can achieve in order to reach that main goal.

I'm a big fan of reaching a goal and attaining that next level in my business. I think one of the things I like about this part of having my own business is that all the rules are laid out before you reach your next goal or level because you've picked up valuable skills along the way. What I've found out is that you can master any goal as long as you don't quit or get discouraged.

Sometimes in video games you have to do the same task over and over until you get really good at it and can move on to the next task. That might frustrate you at first, but later on that tough skill will seem simple compared to another that you have to learn in order to make it past a future level. And hopefully you'll be able to apply the first skill that you learned in order to help you achieve the next skill needed to move ahead. It's the same in business. You need to get your arcade-level business skills together before you can be a master of the entrepreneur game.

What will be your first step today? How are you going to get that bow tie on your neck or that lemonade in your cup? What's the one thing you can do today with almost no money to get the idea of starting a business out of your head and make it a reality?

All you have to do is simply jot down your business idea in a notebook.

Yes, it really is that simple.

Just as no one can sign your name like you or talk like you do or take your place on picture day, *you* are the only person who can unlock your million-dollar idea. All you need to do is simply write it down and start listing your goals so you can be successful.

Back when I first started my business, I didn't know where to begin. Now, if I could go back and tell myself one thing, it would be this: start today. You'll never know what you can gain experience from if you don't simply start. Most people who get into business go to college, and then they attend three more years of business school. I hope for their sake that in those seven years as a student, they also start their own side business so they can be a little ahead of things. I'm running my own company already, and I haven't even been making ties for nine years!

Let's talk about new ways for you to see how to make your ideas work even better for you.

First, you must ask yourself: What are you offering with your business? What is it about your product or service that people can only get from you? This might be a label or a unique service, such as lawn mowing and hedge trimming for the same price. Where can you sell your product so you can set your business apart from others?

For our BOWS this chapter, let's focus on how quickly you can recover from your first attempts at success.

BELIEVE in yourself! Whether you're doing your first farmers' market or lemonade stand, just promise yourself that whatever happens, you will learn from it. Then you try again and succeed by using what you learned.

OPPORTUNITIES to give back are so crucial at the beginning. If you want to be a chef, start by making dinner for your family.

WORK HARD! If it were easy, someone would have done it already.

SEEK SUPPORT from friends and family because they will have your back no matter what. Sometimes you need your family to be kind, and sometimes you can count on them for feedback that you couldn't get from anyone else. Even during the process of writing this book, I used the BOWS every single day. To put it simply: I'd rather hear how to change this book for the better from a loved one early on than from a reviewer when it's too late.

Once you find out what makes you unique, you can find out what will make you excel in your industry.

6

MEASURE YOUR RESOURCES

Now you've come to the fun part! Half the work that entrepreneurs like you do consists of finding resources. I know that I went to school with a few kids who always seemed like they had money for lunch and snacks and who always had new clothes. At times I even thought their parents did their homework because it was always done on time and perfectly.

These kids always seemed to have *resources*. But what if I told you that always having unlimited resources is a bad thing for entrepreneurs? The most important skill you can build from running your own business is learning to be *resourceful*. That doesn't mean being full of resources but, rather, being good at finding them.

Money might seem like the best resource you could have as an entrepreneur, but let's take a look at that with a quick example.

When I started Mo's Bows, I knew I wanted a high-quality product for boys and men. But if that's where I jumped into things, think of all the things I would have had to buy:

- expensive fabric
- sewing lessons
- sewing machine of my own
- scissors
- thread to match every bow tie I made

Just that alone would have cost me about $1,000 (remember, *I* was my first customer, and it took me a couple of months to sell even one bow tie for $5). And what if I bought all that stuff in the list above and then found out I lacked the passion to pursue my business? Now you're talking about a $1,005 loss. For that price, I could have taken my mom and me to Disney World.

But instead of jumping right into business headfirst, and before I spent a single cent, I evaluated my BOWS of Business. I didn't know a thing about sewing, but I did **believe** in myself. I found **opportunities** to give back while I **worked hard** to get good at making bow ties for my friends and family.

I also asked for **support** from my family, and that helped me to find even more resources. It didn't take Granny Cora long to give me my very own sewing machine, after she saw how passionate and dedicated I truly was about fashion and making ties. She also introduced me to people who knew people with unique thread colors and even more scraps of cool fabric for me to use. If I had tried to source all of these **materials** myself, I would have ended up buying two hundred feet of thread when I only needed two feet.

All of the resources you attain as an entrepreneur increase the **value** of your product. Everything is worth what people are willing to pay. But the flip side is that many people have resources that they don't value as much as you do, and that's where you can use your entrepreneurial skills to get those resources for your use.

My granny doesn't like to waste anything, so she has a habit of saving scraps of fabric when she sews clothes for people. She's been doing that for years, and after such a long time, all those loose ends of thread and scrap pieces of fabric didn't matter much to her. If she moved to a new house, she probably wouldn't have valued the box of scraps enough to bring it with her. But for me those scraps, along with her expertise and the use of her sewing machine, were worth more than $1,000. And with those resources, I was able to start my business without spending so much as $1.

Throughout history, some of the greatest entrepreneurs started just like you and me—not with abundant resources but rather with a unique ability to find them. Bill Gates, for example, became one of the richest people on the planet after starting at a young age by using his school rummage-sale proceeds to buy computing time from General Electric. When that money ran out, Gates offered to exchange computing time for helping a local company find bugs in their software. Another local company hired him to write their payroll software and even paid him royalties while he was still in high school. Within months, Gates wrote a computer program to help his school schedule classes. By the time he dropped out of Harvard, he already had more experience with software than any other person his age. This helped him develop a software company that made billions. (As a side note: To buy a computer at that time would have cost hundreds of thousands of dollars. But it didn't really cost GE that much to let some kids use theirs on the weekends. That shows how Gates found the resources he needed in order to attain his goals—all for free!)

Just like with Bill Gates's story, the magic part of entrepreneurship is finding what resources you might have right in front of you and then using them to your full advantage. Entrepreneurs like you are born with the itch to make your lives better and to connect with your families and communities, but businesspeople don't always know how to scratch that itch. Bill Gates is such a good example of the BOWS philosophy. No one his age could afford a computer or program one, but he **believed** in himself and learned. He couldn't afford the computing time, but he offered his expertise as an **opportunity** to give back. He **worked hard** in addition to all of his schoolwork, and when he didn't know how to ask for the things he needed, he would **seek support** from friends and family. And with that he started one of the biggest companies in history. Keep that in mind as you begin your journey as an entrepreneur: right now you might be so focused on that dollar in your pocket that you're missing the million-dollar opportunity within your grasp.

AVOID "ANALYSIS PARALYSIS"

Let's talk for a minute about a problem every entrepreneur will have to learn to solve. You want your ideas to be so successful that you might be afraid to take the leap and to just jump into your business. You might be so passionate about the business you want to start that you can't stand the idea of doing it poorly.

"Analysis paralysis" could lead you to decide that you will never get your business off the ground without enough money to invest in it up front. Instead of focusing on why one idea will or will not work with the resources you can control, try thinking about things using a lemonade stand as an example. With very little money you can run a lemonade stand, use the money from that to run another one, and then flip and invest that into the business of your dreams. Really, it could be that simple!

Even better, running a lemonade stand will teach you everything you need to know about business and how you, as an entrepreneur, can easily solve problems. But how would you start a lemonade stand without any money? Let's figure this out together so you can see how easy it is to jump into your business without access to all your resources up front.

Lemonade-Stand Requirements

- sugar
- ice
- cups
- lemons

If you don't have any money, it might seem hopeless for you to start your lemonade stand. But someone in your family might have a pound of sugar in a kitchen cabinet. They may have paid five dollars for it and forgotten it was even there. What if the expiration date was approaching? Technically, that family member might want to throw out the sugar next week and buy another pound of sugar that will last longer. So it's likely that your family member won't *value* their sugar at the full five dollars. Let's say they're going away for the weekend and won't get to use *any* of that sugar in time before it expires. You can simply ask for it, and I bet you'll get that sugar for free.

The next ingredient you need is ice. Just like in the Bill Gates example above (or even in the case of my grandmother's sewing machine), it's silly to go out and buy your own freezer just to get a couple of ice cubes. You don't need the machine—you need the product made by the machine. Bill Gates didn't need an expensive computer the size of my kitchen just to learn how to code. Even *I* didn't need a sewing machine at first. All you need is someone else who has a freezer where you can make and keep a few ice cubes.

The next item you need is cups. You might find that some people in your family already have paper cups or even reusable plastic cups left over from a party. If you ask, you'll likely be able to use these. There you have it—free cups!

Let's check in with our list:

- ✔ sugar
- ✔ ice
- ✔ cups
- ✔ lemons

Are we stuck, or are we *almost there*? It's a common question.

How come we're keeping the lemons for last? Isn't that the most important ingredient for lemonade? Well, this gets to the heart of what it means to be an entrepreneur. Most people would sit around waiting for lemons to magically appear before they decided to get into the lemonade business. But as an entrepreneur, you must *put yourself in the position* so that you are ready to go the *second* life gives you lemons. Why? Because every other resource you have, you put on hold when you need to. Sugar, ice, and cups can last much longer than lemons because fruit is perishable. It can start to go bad right away if you don't use it.

What I'm saying is something you probably already know: Don't *wait* for the perfect time to start your journey as an entrepreneur. The *last* thing you want is to get a perfect opportunity and end up having to waste it because you didn't have your business set up correctly and ready to go.

In the fashion world designers have to think like this all the time. The fruits in this case are the trends and colors of the season. Designers need to be in position with their designs and patterns so that they can deal with what's in season the minute it hits the runway.

Once you get further along in your journey toward starting your own business, you might have to start thinking about taking on investors. Early on, when you are starting your entrepreneurial journey, your investors are likely your friends and family. They invest time in showing you where to get resources, in driving you to places where you can get supplies, and in helping you carry things to your lemonade stand. Don't worry—you'll be able to pay them back once you're the CEO of your own company someday. Investors typically like to help solve problems and to get people they are passionate about or believe in on the right track to succeed in their venture. For **angel investors**, the problem they usually solve is a lack of money for starting a business or service. And that's what you need to find in order to make your lemonade stand a reality.

Not all of us can be investors. But many of your family members know a bargain when they see one. People willing to help you out are taking on the *risk* because they see how hard you hustled to get all the other resources in line to make your stand run. They might even respect that you insist on using fresh lemons in your final product.

It's likely that most anyone who cares about you will be willing to lend you a dollar for the lemons you need as long as you pay them back as soon as you sell your first glass of lemonade (for a dollar). And the twenty-nine glasses you'll sell after that? That's twenty-nine dollars in pure profit for you to use on another venture.

Think about the business you want to start. What are the "lemons" preventing you from beginning today? More important, *How can you get everything in order so that when the lemons you need turn up, you are ready to go?*

For the end of this chapter, I want to do something just slightly different. Let's use the BOWS of Business to see where you are successful and where you can improve in your hypothetical lemonade stand.

BELIEVE in yourself! If you got your lemonade stand off the ground today with zero supplies and no main ingredient, you're killing it!

OPPORTUNITIES to give back. In the next few chapters you'll revisit the lemonade stand and see how you can use it to enrich your family and community.

WORK HARD! What's a lemonade stand without lemons? This is an opportunity to work on your resourcefulness.

SEEK SUPPORT from friends and family. Here you secured your first angel investor, raised **capital**, and even made good on your first loan by paying your investor back after your very first sale.

7

EARN WHAT
YOU LEARN!

Some part of you right now may find yourself in "analysis paralysis" mode. You've got the resources to make thirty cups of lemonade, so you have everything you need to begin your business. But as an entrepreneur, you're used to doing things your own way—putting your own spin on things. Maybe you have a particular style or aesthetic that you want to get across in your lemonade business before you go public with it. That's good and commendable. But I'm going to give you permission right now to put a pause on perfection.

Everything that will make you successful in the future will come from what you learn by simply testing and trying (and making mistakes, of course). Is this part of starting a business scary? Yes. But you know what else is scary? Roller coasters. Thinking about becoming an entrepreneur is like waiting in line for a roller coaster. It makes your stomach flutter a little anticipating the ride. But starting your own business is like that part of the roller coaster when you begin to slowly climb the first hill. Parts of you kinda want to just stop the whole thing and get off. However, the fun part of riding a roller coaster or starting a business is taking the leap!

It took me a long time to figure out that the gap between wanting something better and making something better is large. This is where most people who think they want to start a business give up because they don't like not knowing how something is going to turn out and if mistakes are going to be made. They go through life always feeling like they're on the way up that first hill of the roller coaster. But I promise you that once you take that leap—once you get over the first hill—you can't even *think* about how you used to feel. You're too busy enjoying the ride!

The key to filling your life with more roller-coaster-ride moments is to just get past your scared feeling. To do that you simply need to make more stuff. If you want to be an inventor, draw out everything you want to invent. If you want to be a designer, make sure you make something every day. You need practice. You need to be patient with yourself. And above all, just keep going!

It's really *that* simple. I don't make great bow ties because I always made great bow ties; I make great bow ties because I made *so many bad ones first*. And in that time of experimenting and perfecting my product, I learned all the tricks that would later make my job feel like second nature to me.

One final important thing in this section to note is that you don't measure just to start your business. It's a cycle. In your lemonade stand you will measure out your ingredients, cut the lemons, and stitch it all together in a pitcher. But once you see your product out there, you'll find that it's time to measure again. Is your lemonade too sweet? Too lemony? Can you make one gallon as easily as you can make ten gallons? You can probably guess that I'm going to tell you not to wait for the perfect recipe to come your way. If you can get your business up and running with a simple recipe, then good. Just remember to keep improving it until you have one you can make that you can *really* sell! Don't be afraid to *measure* what makes you so successful, even if you have to do so a few times before you reach perfection.

Use your friends and family as your *beta testers* for your special lemonade product. Beta testers can become part of a group known in business as *early adopters*. They are a group who loves having opinions, and they get a lot out of seeing what other people might call unfinished work. Early adopters get the most bragging rights in the future. If someone asks your friends about your lemonade business, your friends might proudly tell that person, "It's great to be Dave's friend because he lets me try all the new flavors before anyone else does." The feedback early adopters give you can be used to improve the quality of your product.

Going back to the early days of my bow tie business, my classmates from school loved to see me on TV talking about my product *because* they remembered when I made them their first ones out of scrap fabric. It's a story they like to tell. For that reason, right now I would ask our hypothetical lemonade-stand owners to go ahead and try out some new flavors.

How's the first glass? It might taste pretty bad! And that's okay. Right now you're not wasting resources; you're **product testing**. This is when it helps to have family and friends you can count on and when it's important that you not take your early reviews personally, but rather think about the critiques and then work on perfecting your product accordingly.

Your goal now should be to collect as many opinions as possible and not worry about what criticism you may receive. Imagine having a windshield between you and what people say about your lemonade. The first person says it's sweet; another says it's too watery. Maybe one of them is right. The key now is to get more feedback so you can make sure you are providing the best possible product for your business to succeed.

Just like putting the sugar before the lemons, you want people's input *before* you can feel confident in knowing you can pull off your business. Think back to the notion that most entrepreneurs want to keep their business plans to themselves, especially at the beginning. The reason is so that no one else can steal their idea.

But because the success of your venture comes down to how you pull everything together, you don't have to give away any of your moves even while beta testing your product. That way, by the time someone else maybe decides that your idea is worth pursuing, you'll be miles ahead.

The truth is, most lemonade recipes are the same. But the reason you see so many different brands of lemonade out there is due to **marketing**. In the next few chapters we'll talk about what marketing is and why it's so important in making your business a success.

THE END OF
PART 1

This brings us to the end of "Measure." So far you have learned to upend what the "experts" in your life might say and to find free resources that will put you way ahead of your competition. All that's missing now is your first product. Trust me: Make it, take pictures of it, and try it out today for the first time. Years from now, when you run your own corporate empire, you can post that first picture in the lobby of your company, and customers or investors waiting to meet with you will know just how far you've come.

What I'd like to do before you go on to the next part is to reflect on your BOWS of Business for the first part of the book. If you were Karen or Dave starting your lawn-mowing business or lemonade stand and got stuck, what would you do? You would probably work your way out of those tricky situations by using BOWS of Business to keep moving toward those goals. Apply these tips and tricks to your own business when you find yourself stuck in a rut or unable to move forward due to some obstacle.

BELIEVE in yourself! Karen and Dave started with nothing. But they worked on their pitches and on their sales and product techniques. What could you do to help boost your confidence in yourself and your business?

OPPORTUNITIES to give back! Whether it was handing out samples or looking for volunteer opportunities, Karen and Dave never stopped building their community of support. You must constantly reach out to the community to draw in new and repeat customers and to get the buzz going about your business.

WORK HARD! Mowing lawns or selling lemonade is work. But look at all the extra work that went into it. Could Karen and Dave just get a job where someone else pays them to mow lawns or make lemonade? Yeah, but as an entrepreneur, you put in the work regardless of the resources in front of you because you are following your goal and your passion. Is there work you could put in right now to help you move forward in the near future?

SEEK SUPPORT from friends and family. Whether Karen needed to borrow a family member's lawn mower or Dave needed to borrow money from his mom for lemons, they needed support and feedback from family and friends—and you do, too. Have you thought of family members you could ask to help you get your business off the ground?

In the next two parts you are going to improve on these ideas and then improve on them again. If you want more time with Part 1, give it a reread before moving on. You also might find it helpful to keep going because all that we have talked about will come up again and again as we measure everything we know and take our biggest leap together!

CUT

In Part 1, you learned how to gather materials and then figured out what you could make (this is what I have been referring to as "measure"). In this next part you will take what you gathered in "Measure" and learn how to "cut" it down to size. What a lot of business owners learn along the way is how they could have been more efficient from the start. That is an important part of any business, but in my experience, *learning* how to become more efficient comes from learning how you work best.

Be warned: you will learn to make a lot of cuts in this next section.

I want to give you a quick example of why cutting is so important to learn for your business. We'll call this example the "Bow Tie Wednesday Problem." After all the pain of learning how to make just one bow tie, I had kids at school asking me if I could make one for them. I had a lot of great scrap fabric to use, and my mom and granny volunteered to help me. I had an "initial order" of twenty bow ties. This was an **opportunity** to give back with a capital O!

Using the BOWS of Business, I had to first **believe** in myself and my abilities as an entrepreneur. I had the fabric, I had an order for twenty bow ties, and I even had my mom and granny to help me measure, cut, and stitch them together.

Many people might suggest that my mom, granny, and I should divide up the work—maybe Mom could measure, Mo could cut, and

Granny could stitch. And this is how we started, but we soon found that caused more problems for us than it solved. It actually wasted more time than was necessary. While one of us was measuring the fabric, the other two had nothing to do so we just sat around, waiting. We also started wasting some of our precious fabric and thread as well.

In the end we found that it took *less* time for each of us to find the right fabric, check whether we had enough of the right color thread, measure out one single bow tie, and then stitch it together.

Whether it's the lemons in your family's fridge or the lawn mower that gets used only once a week, once you learn to *measure* your resources you can see that there are opportunities all around you. The important thing is to have the guts to pursue these opportunities. The only way to do that is to "*cut*" your resources into usable pieces that will move your business forward. Where to cut, how to cut, and how to make better cuts is what you will learn in this next section.

The key is to be entrepreneurs at every level of your business. I learned a lot from trying to make my first bow tie, so why shouldn't I learn even more from making my first batch of ties? If you are engaged and willing to learn from your mistakes—to make cuts where necessary—you are sure to be much more successful in your business as a whole. So grab those scissors and let's begin!

8

BUILDING
RELATIONSHIPS

t's time to focus on product development. However, the product I want to work on before anything else is actually *you*.

"But, Mo," you might ask, "how can I be a product when I'm trying to *sell* a product?" Great question! Remember back to the beginning of the book and this quote by Professor Howard Stevenson of Harvard Business School: *"Entrepreneurship is the pursuit of opportunity without regard to resources currently controlled."*

When you ask someone to invest in your business, you are really asking them to invest in you. Whether you provide a truly unique product or service (like my bow ties) or you are in a crowded market (like lawn mowing or lemonade making), the biggest selling point of your business is *you*.

You've probably heard your parents or teachers tell you to speak up or to stop mumbling or to stand up straight at one time or another. Usually, that's just adults being adults. But what if I told you that you can make other people *want* to invest in your business just by the way you walk and talk and present yourself to the world? The more confidence you show, the more likely you'll be to get people to want to invest in you and your company because they'll feel that you are professional and know exactly what you are doing.

How can you build confidence and present yourself like a true businessperson? The first step is to have a great way of introducing yourself and meeting people. And the easiest way to get over your introduction jitters is to have your *"Shark Tank* pitch" worked out (see Chapter 4 for a refresher on this). You may feel self-conscious the first time you give your pitch to someone you've just met. That's okay! I did, too. But your pitch will get easier each time you practice, and each time you'll feel more and more confident in yourself and what you are selling.

You should also consider what drives you to want to be an entrepreneur. For me, I saw a hole in the market that could be filled with my bow ties. I didn't have the closest relationships with my dad and granddad, but I did love seeing old photos of them dressed up. I wanted to have a connection to them through the fashion I wore, but the kids' bow ties I found in stores looked so cheap. I couldn't find high-quality, handmade bow ties made specifically for kids. So I saw an opportunity to grow a business, and I went for it. I didn't know a lot about business, but I got to start working with my mom and my granny to make my dream a reality.

What about you? What makes you want to be an entrepreneur? Maybe you are saving up for a new bike or for college. Maybe you want to start a side business that will help you raise money for another opportunity down the road. If you ask Karen and Dave why they didn't just get a job mowing lawns or selling lemonade at the mall, what would they say? I bet if you asked every entrepreneur why they want to be in business, they would each give you a unique answer. That's what makes entrepreneurs special: their stories behind why they went into business for themselves.

As an entrepreneur you are always out there selling yourself. Since *you* are your main product and entrepreneurs are always looking for ways to improve their product line, let's do some product development *on you*.

Let's talk about how to get your uniqueness across when you introduce yourself to others:

1. **Smile!** Everybody likes seeing a happy person. And if you have trouble thinking of something to smile about, just remember that anyone you meet might just be *the* person to help you pursue your dreams and grow your business.

2. **Speak up!** Grown-ups can't always hear kids when they talk casually. So talk like grown-ups do—nice and loud! Speaking loudly and clearly when you introduce your business plan to people tells them that you know exactly what you're talking about. It shows that you have confidence and that you have thought a lot about your business as well.

3. **Care about your appearance!** I've always believed that when you look good, you feel good. You will make a big impression on others if you look put together when talking about your business. And that, in turn, will make them

feel good about listening to your pitch. Looking good can mean a lot of different things to a lot of different people, so a good rule to follow is to always dress for the job you want to get. Many people think entrepreneurs are just home in their underwear and flip-flops sending emails on their laptop. But a real entrepreneur wants to be out there putting together new deals, reaching new customers, and growing new businesses.

To try it out on yourself, go ahead and take your picture in three different outfits: your school clothes, your pajamas, and your fanciest outfit. Then look at the pictures and ask yourself, *Which one of these kids would I hire if I met them in person or saw them online today?*

4. **Have a firm handshake!** I can't believe this one works, but it really does (and it's super important in making a good first impression). A firm handshake is like catching someone with an element of surprise. It seals the deal, as we say in business. When you are dealing with grown-ups who have never worked with a young entrepreneur before, they will likely be skeptical that you can really do everything you claim to be able or want to do. But giving them a firm handshake will let them know you've done this before and that you have the confidence of a strong businessperson. Trust me: a firm handshake will help others put their faith in you and whatever it is you are selling or wanting to pursue.

5. **Have a passionate attitude about your product!** Maybe to some people your product looks simply like a bow tie

or a glass of lemonade. But people don't want something plain or ordinary—they want something extraordinary! This is where everything you've been working on comes together. You've got a cool brand with a great backstory, you're putting yourself out there, and—BAM!—you've got an exceptional product and you *just can't wait* to tell others about it.

Now, you may be worrying that your pitch will sound phony or that you'll appear to be bragging when you share your backstory, but it's not bragging if you can back it up with solid ideas and product. People *love* to talk about finding new products and services before anybody else does. Think about how much further along you will get in your business if *every* customer turns around and tells five friends what an amazing experience they had with you and your product?

It's *okay* to be a little uncomfortable with selling yourself and your brand at first. But how about this? You only have to do it right once. Imagine that you went door to door in your neighborhood, slouching and mumbling while trying to sell your lawn-mowing service. Let's say you had to do this six times. Six *painful* times.

Now imagine that you did it right *once*:

1. You went out there and you put on a big smile.
2. You spoke nice and loud.
3. You took pride in your appearance.
4. You gave the customer a firm handshake.
5. You shared your passion for your product.

That person will likely turn around and tell five friends about you and your lawn-mowing service, and they may all end up calling you to come handle their lawns. Suddenly, you have *six* customers just by talking effectively to one. And the dominoes keep falling, and you keep getting additional customers via word of mouth. It really can be *that* simple—all because you went out there with confidence in yourself and your product. And the best part is that it didn't cost you a thing.

All you need to do to start getting your business out there is to BELIEVE in yourself, look for OPPORTUNITIES to give back, WORK HARD, and SEEK SUPPORT from friends and family. Follow the BOWS of Business like always. I promise, it's really that simple.

CHAPTER

9

ZERO-DOLLAR
MARKETING

As my mom and I entered the *Shark Tank* stage, I knew that even I could be just any kid starting a small fashion line. But all it would take to get my business to the next level would be to make a connection with just one of the Sharks. So when I started my pitch, instead of talking at length about what my bow ties were made of, I told the Sharks about *how* they got made. I told them the story of my mom, Granny, and me. I said, "Sharks, I always, I mean always, like to dress nice. Even when I was little, I would wear a suit and tie just to go play on the playground. But the problem was I couldn't find any bow ties that I liked. So my grandma showed me how to sew. And then, Mo's Bows became—" Only then I blanked out again. No matter how many times I gave my pitch, I wasn't prepared for how they would react.

When all of them looked up at me, I put on my biggest smile of the day and continued because my mom and I always agreed what my last line would be: "Who's coming with me?" They couldn't keep the smiles from their faces. Barbara Corcoran finally spoke up: "I feel like I'm watching Daymond John standing right before me."

Everyone looked at Daymond, and I could tell that when he looked at me, he did see a bit of himself. I'm young, I'm full of passion, and I mean every word I say. The only difference between me and Daymond is thirty years.

That's the moment I started thinking that there was no way he'd be able to pass on me.

Making a connection between your product and your customers is *so* critical to your success. As an entrepreneur, you have to remember one very key thing: *you* are the product. Marketing is all about how to get your product to stand out in a crowded consumer space. But how you get your customer to reach out and select *your* product is the final step. It's also the hardest. It also pays off the most if you succeed.

In this chapter we're going to get into how you can market your business and create your Zero-Dollar Advertising Budget.

The number-one thing your business needs in order to succeed is to tell a great story. No matter how many times I tell my business story, I never get tired of it. And people seem to never get tired of hearing it.

When you look at the most successful companies, they're always the ones with the best stories. A lot of companies make smartphones, and they have a lot of different uses. People will always have their own preferences in the smartphone market.

But people love to tell the story of Apple's founder Steve Jobs and his friends hiding out in his parents' garage, bringing the power of computing to the masses. That's why so many people choose to buy iPhones over other smartphones.

What's your business's story? It's okay if the story hasn't been written yet. But (hint, hint) everything you learned in "Measure" will help you tell a story that people will love.

As an example, let me tell you two stories:

1. Karen built a lemonade stand to make some money on the weekends. She found the supplies and built a desk and printed out a big sign. It rained a little the day she set up her stand, which ruined her sign, but she still sold her lemonade. At the end of the day, she had enough money saved to get a new sign made for the next time she set up the stand.

2. When Suzy's grandmother was sick in the hospital, her family decided to run a ten-mile road race to raise money for cancer research. Suzy was too young to run, so she started a lemonade stand to support her family *and* raise money for cancer research. She set up her stand at the end of the race route, and even though it rained on the day of the race, she still made money.

Which one of these stories sticks with you?

Now, the stories above are somewhat dramatic examples. Karen represents the kind of businessperson you want to deal with, but you are likely more willing to identify with the second story because it tells you something about the origin of the

business and also gives you a sense, as a consumer, of where your money is going.

In crafting your story, you can absolutely pick from your BOWS of Business for details. You started this journey because you BELIEVE in yourself. While you got started, you looked for OPPORTUNITIES to give back. You WORK HARD, and you have SUPPORT from your friends and family. All you have to do is flesh out the details, and there you have it—your business now has a killer and honest story.

Next, you need to practice telling your story. Keep it really, really short. You know when someone gets started on a story and it seems to take longer than the events themselves? You will know when you have told a good story because people will easily tell it to each other. Think back to the two lemonade-stand examples above. The two stories take just as long to tell. Suzy and Karen both had to put in the same amount of work for their businesses, and they even made the same product. But which lemonade stand would you rather go to and buy your l emonade from?

In my business I know that once stores start selling bow ties, other bow tie companies will likely catch on. What can I do to stop both the store managers and the customers from buying those other bow ties? Nothing. What can I do to get the stores and their customers to buy *my* bow ties instead? Everything. I always guarantee that everything I make is of the highest quality and at the best price. Also, when people buy one of my bow ties, they also buy a little piece of the story of a kid with a dream who got help from his family to start a thriving business. I tell the story of my business every day.

Can you guess how I learned to tell people my story? It's

about a kid who learned to BELIEVE in himself, he looked for OPPORTUNITIES to give back, he WORKED HARD, and he got SUPPORT from friends and family.

Five years from now, will you be able to say the same about your business? Perfect your story, help make it impactful to your customer, and hopefully you will!

CHAPTER

10

SOCIAL MEDIA
GUIDE

O
ne thing that makes start-ups different from other business is that they have what is called a "global scale." That means that the business has the ability to expand almost anywhere in the world. This makes start-ups just a little different from a lemonade stand that can cover only one block or a lawn-mowing business that is limited to the lawns you can easily get to.

Think back to that first custom white bow tie I made for a friend at school. On that day Mo's Bows had its first paying customer. I couldn't make a custom bow tie for every person on the globe. But at that time, what I offered had a customer base in my area that was ready for my product. Your business may start out the same way, and that's great! But that's the reason you need to go find your customers—and you can do that by establishing and building up your social media presence.

Even though I had a great story to share with people about

the creation of Mo's Bows, it still took a lot of work to get it out there. Memphis, where I live, has nice clothing stores, but soon my mom and I had visited them all. People would tell me that a growing business must be "scalable," meaning that if you can make ten of something, you should be able to make one hundred or even one thousand. But if all of this is based on just one person's efforts, you can't grow because you can't **scale** by just yourself. I like to remind other entrepreneurs that *you can't scale a person*.

But you *can scale* a story by sharing it on social media.

When I started Mo's Bows, I had done some local new stories about the company, but that wasn't enough to get the word out about my product in a large way. So I set up Facebook and Instagram accounts for my business, and that's where I was able to share the story about me and about Mo's Bows with a larger consumer base.

I'm so glad I started my business in the age of social media. It's no doubt a huge reason for my success. In fact, my first national TV appearance on *The Steve Harvey Show* came about from the show's wardrobe stylist, who saw my Facebook page. And even now, five years after being on the show, many of my customers tell me that's where they first heard about Mo's Bows. The clip has been shared and viewed on social media thousands of times, giving people the opportunity to share my story with like-minded individuals. I noticed an immediate increase in followers, website traffic, and sales after this TV appearance aired.

To get a sense of where people are hearing about your business, it's a good idea to ask those who send you requests for products or appearances to ask how they heard about you. For example, whenever I get a request to appear on a show or speak at an event, I always ask the program coordinator where they heard about me and Mo's Bows. A lot of the time, people respond that they follow Mo's Bows on Instagram and love what my business is doing. When we first started, we made a big splash. But soon everybody in my school who wanted a bow tie had already gotten one from me. Through social media we could scale our brand to find stylish young people all over the world. Many people who are new to business feel that they have to advertise their company using TV commercials or in magazine and newspaper ads. And that's really expensive, especially for a start-up. Social media, on the other hand, is often free and can reach even more people than a more traditional ad. So don't neglect to get your business up and online via various social media channels, and be sure you are frequently engaged with your consumers, other businesses, and young entrepreneurs on your account so it stays relevant and in the public eye.

One of the best ways to do this is by giving your social media followers something of value—whether it's an update on your company, a new sale, a followers-only special, or a tip based on your expertise. That way people will want to keep up with you as you grow. This is another reason having a great story is a huge benefit. People want to know what happens next!

The Internet is a very visual place, so you want to make sure that your social media accounts tell your story through great pictures. Shortly after I set up Mo's Bows, I was lucky enough to be introduced to a young, talented photographer who believed in my vision and wanted to see me succeed. By using great photography, the photographer was able to tell a story about my company on social media that was like no other. But since most of us will benefit from social media first, I'm going to share with you everything I've learned from working with professional photographers. So here is the Mo's Bows Guide to Taking Awesome Pictures for Your Business's Social Media Pages:

1. **Make your product stand out!** When people scroll through social media accounts, you need to give them a reason to stop and look at yours. So consider the following when taking pictures:
   - Use vibrant colors.
   - Make sure the object you are photographing is in focus.
   - Clear out other objects from the area where you are shooting the photo.
   - Make sure there isn't any ketchup or mustard on your shirt if you will be in the photo!

2. **Make the photo the best it can be!** The reason people go to expensive photo studios for a modeling shoot is not because the camera is there, but because the expensive lighting is there. You can reenact good lighting at home, however, by paying attention to the following:
   - Bring your product over to the window for that perfect photo lighting. It's lighting for free! North-facing windows are best so you avoid your product being backlit or too washed out.
   - Place the back of your phone or camera against the window.
   - Zoom in so that the background is a little out of focus.
   - Then snap away!

Sharing your story on social media and on your business's website is very important, but what's also crucial to any

HANDCRAFTED
MO'S BOWS
BOW TIES
&
EST. 2011

storytelling is to show, don't tell! The people who want to know more about your product will follow, subscribe, like, and comment on all your posts. When that happens, it tells the social network site that people like seeing posts from you. The algorithms that run social media sites like Instagram favor active users. So a popular post is likely to get more popular, and even *more* people will see your future posts after that.

But how do you get more post engagement? Here are a few tips:

1. **Engage with your followers!**
   - Ask questions and respond to the answers in the comments.
   - Be yourself! People follow your brand because they want to know more about you. Post regular photos of you doing your thing alongside your business photos, so your followers (and potential customers) learn more about you through your interests.

2. **Location, Location, Location!**
   - Use the location tag to highlight local businesses, parks, and even your hometown when you are posting photos.
   - If your photo stands out and has the most comments and likes, it will shoot to the top rated and help you gain more exposure.

3. **Establish rituals to keep them coming back!**
   - Hashtags are your friend. Use them and reuse them to establish something unique for your account. For example:

- I started a hashtag on Instagram when I first joined, and I continue to keep up that tradition of #bowtietuesday each week.
- When I want to share quotes that have helped me, I give them on #motivationalmondays.
- To encourage my customers to interact with each other, we also have everybody #showmoyourbow.

Even if you're just starting your business, get your social media presence going right away. Just from people finding my social media pages, I have since partnered with St. Jude, March of Dimes, and the Boys and Girls Club to make custom bow ties for their organizations. People find me through my company's website, and they always tell me that they follow me on social media.

As to how to get started: Get going with your BOWS of Business, of course!

BELIEVE in your story and your brand.

Know that OPPORTUNITIES to share that story are all around you. But they grow when they become opportunities to give back.

WORK HARD. You will improve over time. Get ready to see how far you've come. Remember the best #throwbackthursday photos are equal parts embarrassing and adorable. Think of Steve Jobs in the garage. Your business will have a bright future only if you give it a great past.

SEEK SUPPORT from friends and family. All I'll say is that my mom is a very patient photographer.

CHAPTER

11

QUICK AND EASY
WAYS TO GO VIRAL

I guarantee that you will never forget the first time someone stops you in the street and says, "Hey, aren't you that guy [or girl] who runs that business I keep hearing about?"

Once people start recognizing you and your product, you are on your way to killing it with your business. When people engage with you on a business level, you know what you're doing is working. Your customers know they can count on you to do a great job. You have your social media established and have taken the time to tell the story of your company.

Now, you need help growing your business to the next level. And you can do that absolutely free just by generating press via word of mouth.

I think we all have a friend who secretly hopes he or she will go viral someday. But did you know that most viral stories have a few things in common? Advertisers have spent a lot of time and money trying to figure this out, and the incredible thing is that even though advertisers pay people millions of dollars, you don't need to spend a lot of money to make your business go viral. It really just comes down to three things:

1. tastemakers
2. communities
3. surprise

The following sections will explain more about these three key ingredients to making your business go viral and to expanding your customer base.

TASTEMAKERS

When I started my company, I had very few customers (mainly just family and friends), but I continued to work hard and someone told a friend of theirs at the local news station about Mo's Bows. The producer at the station decided to have me on the show. After that aired, someone shared my story on Facebook and with the wardrobe stylist on *The Steve Harvey Show,* and he shared it with the producer of his show. They thought it would be of some value to see a young entrepreneur with that classic swag on their show.

But what did Steve Harvey value? Anyone who has seen his show knows he likes nice clothes. Yet what he values more than that is his audience. It took me a long time to really understand this. Steve Harvey knew that people all over the country love to hear great stories about how different kinds of families change their lives for the better by relying on each other. That's definitely the case with the story of Mo's Bows. (Out of all the stories he gets every day, it didn't hurt that my story *also* involved nice clothes, of course.)

See how quickly, and without much work at all on my part, my business went from my mother telling a friend about Mo's Bows to my going on national television? Now imagine how many other big tastemakers watched that show. Spreading the word about your business and going viral are not about one person sharing your story; rather, that happens when many different people from all over feel the need to share your story with others. That way when a tastemaker is impressed with your work, they will be impressed by how many people saw it before they did.

COMMUNITIES

Thanks to the Internet, there seems to be a community for just about anyone or anything online. Whether it's selling kids'

fashion or fancy juices, young entrepreneurs can more easily find the communities they are targeting with their businesses. And as soon as you as a young entrepreneur can find *your* community of people who will be interested in what you are doing, the sooner you can start spreading your story within that community, hoping for it to snowball and fan out to an even larger customer reach or to investors seeking what you are selling.

You can get a sense of this by following new, cool, and fresh accounts online. I found my community by following celebrities who are fashion influencers and advocates for giving back. I find myself drawn to the community of people who appreciate life, fashion, art, *and* family and who are not afraid to be themselves without making excuses.

The most vital part of accessing communities is how much smarter you can work with an audience that wants to hear what you have to say. Imagine these two scenarios:

1. I go door to door to every house in my neighborhood to see if there is anyone who wants to buy bow ties one day.

2. People who follow fashion hashtags stumble upon my page. They follow me now, and then when they need a bow tie, they know where to go.

See how much time you can save just by focusing on finding the right audience online? This is exactly what I did, and by doing so I was able to reach so many different groups of people who had a common interest in my story.

So think about it: How many groups can you appeal to online to try to expand your community?

One amazing thing about your business going viral is that it's pretty hard to copy something that already went viral. That's because *nothing* beats the element of surprise. It's a magical moment that brings everything together. If you follow a certain tastemaker or community, you end up seeing a lot of the same stuff. But *you* can be the secret surprise factor that shows up and changes everything.

The Sharks on *Shark Tank* were so used to seeing middle-aged businesspeople on the show that they couldn't help but listen to my pitch, which was new, fresh, and very different from previous pitches. It was the same for viewers at home.

The reason I share this with you is because it's something within reach to all of you as young entrepreneurs. By having that surprise factor, every viral story is automatically unique. And guess what? So are you!

What's great about a viral story is that it can keep growing. I told the story of my business on a national TV show the same way I would tell a friend or a new customer in person. TV producers wanted to broadcast my story into living rooms across America because stories like mine always *begin* in living rooms. Maybe every family doesn't have a seamstress wiz for a granny, but every family wants their kids to succeed in whatever they set their minds to.

So how about you? Can you think of a great way to tell people about your product? Can you think of any **tastemakers** who will share your story in different **communities**? Perhaps you might be the one in for the real **surprise**!

Hint: if you get stuck, always remember to check in with your BOWS of Business:

BELIEVE the story you are telling is unique to you.

OPPORTUNITIES to share your story will come along if you always look for ways to give back.

WORK HARD and remember that people weren't writing articles about me and interviewing me on TV just because I made one bow tie with my granny's fabric scraps. They were drawn to me and my company because of the unique story of a kid who just kept on pursuing his dream—a story that I share quickly on social media.

SUPPORT from friends and family is key. This is how the word of mouth about your business will spread, so don't be too quick to intervene and ask them to stop talking about you and your "hobby."

12

PUSHING
THE FOUR *P*S

What's crazy is that even after all of this, you will still encounter new challenges. The hustle needed to run your own business is very real! A lot of people with great business ideas and great products fail. Maybe if they could afford a high-priced sales staff or marketing company, they would have more luck. But I have found that you can improve how your product gets out there by working on what I call the Four *P*s: *place, price, promotion,* and *product.*

I'll be honest that, for me, following the Four *P*s didn't go perfectly at first, but you can learn from what I did, so hopefully the Four *P*s will come easily for you and your business!

When I first started trying to expand Mo's Bows to reach more customers, my mom and I used to go store to store to sell our product. Most store managers we met thought we were crazy because no one sold bow ties at my price level. Most stores didn't sell them, period. And the few who did sold cheap-looking ties that seemed like they belonged on a Halloween costume.

My first retail opportunity came in from Shelton Clothiers, a men's clothing store in downtown Memphis. The owner, Tom Shelton, read about me and my company in our local newspaper and reached out to me directly about carrying my product in his store.

Even after Shelton Clothiers started selling my bow ties, though, I still needed a way to make my product stand out in the store. So I took the lessons I'd learned from my days at the farmers' market and set up a special little shop in the store. In the fashion industry this is called a "trunk show." The concept and execution are very simple, since the store handles all the inventory and sales for your product.

Even if I didn't sell a single bow tie, the trunk show would give me other valuable things for my business, such as meeting potential new customers and learning more about their shopping needs and wants. So I went to Shelton Clothiers on a Saturday during the holidays, and as a promotion I launched a specialty holiday bow tie for the season.

We spread the word on social media, and my mom asked all of her friends to come see us. By the time the Mo's Bows display opened, I already had people lined up to hear more about the business and to get their exclusive holiday bow tie.

Later when I tried to figure out what made the trunk show such a success, it all came down to the Four *P*s: *place, price, promotion,* and *product.* I had a great *place*—a store and store owner who believed in me and my bow ties. My *price* point was right in line with the other clothes the store sold. I received great *promotion* from the local newspaper and news station for the trunk

show, and even more just by being present in the store with a good sign and a big smile. But by launching the limited-time holiday *product* only that one day, I made the most of my time in the store.

When using the Four *P*s, you can increase sales by changing your product, promotion, or price. When I started Mo's Bows, I had bow ties made of scrap fabric that didn't take too much time to make, so I made them specially to order. Soon, I could take three scraps of the same fabric and make three bow ties. Since my costs were so low at the start, it made sense for me to give some of my bow ties away in promotions as well. Finally, once I had my first custom order, I started charging a price for my bow ties. When I was ready to expand, I started thinking about the place where I could best sell my ties—and in some cases it was a few different places.

As a young entrepreneur, you have a lot of control over your *product, price, place,* and *promotion.* When you run a big company you will have much different costs than when you are just working by yourself or with family. And since your job as a young entrepreneur is to *learn how to sell better* at all times, you can drastically alter your price and place to offer a better promotion to drive more sales and interest. When I was starting out, my costs were very low. I could afford to offer my product at a very low *price,* or if I had a lot of one color fabric I could make a bunch of bow ties and give them away in a *promotion.*

Let's revisit the BOWS of Business to see where you are now that you are getting your business off the ground. How can you add in the Four *P*s to get new experiences and new customers?

First of all, you have to continue to BELIEVE in yourself. There's not one person on earth who can run your company as well as you can. You're gonna be great!

If it's hard to come up with sales at the beginning—or if you're not comfortable asking for money when you're just starting out—then look for OPPORTUNITIES to give back. Can you run a promotion just for your family and friends to get your product out there?

Always WORK HARD. Your first experiment with the Four *P*s might not be a success. But you'll figure it out eventually, so get ready to be lucky! You never know who might need you tomorrow.

If you need feedback, seek SUPPORT from friends and family. My business, my products, and even my book are the result of dozens and dozens of conversations with my friends and family.

CHAPTER

13

AVOID GETTING
LEFT BEHIND

I t didn't happen overnight and took a few years, but finally Mo's Bows started getting regular customer orders. My mom, Granny, and some family friends all worked hard to keep up with the orders. The phone was ringing with steady business as well as reporters asking to hear more about the company's story and what I was up to next. I used this as an opportunity to tell them about new products and collections that I had coming up, like seasonal lines of ties and new partnership opportunities.

Business picked up so much, in fact, that my mom was actually able to quit her job and focus on the company full-time while I went to school and did my homework during the week. In the beginning, I would often sell just a few ties, spend the money to buy new supplies and materials, and then repeat that cycle. But now, with steady business coming in, my mom and I could really plan the future of Mo's Bows.

Building a business can absolutely feel like an uphill battle, as it takes constant work and dedication to get everything up and running. Once I felt that Mo's Bows had become a rather successful business, the next hurdle was trying not to stagnate on the plateau of "just good enough."

What I mean by getting caught up in the "just good enough" phase of growing your business is that you can quickly start to lose your sharpness as an entrepreneur. I started to worry that if people saw how easy it had been to build Mo's Bows into a relatively successful company, competitors might decide to start their own bow tie business, stealing all that I'd worked hard to establish and create.

So even though I had a great product, a great story, and great customers, I had to essentially start all over to make my business bigger and better (though not from scratch this time, thankfully).

Some of the success you'll see early on as an entrepreneur will come from sheer luck. As an entrepreneur, you'll try to take on unusual challenges to put you in a unique position to find new opportunities. Basically, entrepreneurs make their own luck. But there is a difference between being an entrepreneur and being an opportunist. If it started raining now and you went outside and sold umbrellas, you're really an opportunist. An entrepreneur knows that it will rain again and that people will need umbrellas more than just once. So the entrepreneur spends time on a sunny day to get ready for selling umbrellas when it rains. Maybe the entrepreneur knows that a big football game or festival is scheduled for a rainy day. The entrepreneur will seize that opportunity and leverage it into better opportunities in the future.

For a young entrepreneur, school dances are a great "rainy day" opportunity to sell your product. In my case, I knew that a lot of kids would need bow ties for the dance. I put on my entrepreneur hat and decided that I could offer an exclusive product—like a bow tie in my school's colors—or use this as an opportunity to put some older bow ties on sale in hopes of finding new customers.

But you can also be an entrepreneur about *how* you run your business. For example, Karen with the lawn-mowing business already has a small list of steady customers. If after a big storm she offers to come to her customers' homes to clean up fallen sticks or leaves in their yards, she may increase her business and build even more rapport with her existing customers. Dave with his lemonade stand could set it up along the path of a road race and make more profit in an hour than he would on a typical Saturday setting up a stand outside his house or at the farmers' market.

Karen and Dave put in the hard work up front to establish trust in their product or service within their community. Building good relationships right away allows an entrepreneur to then be able to adapt to new situations that may help increase their business down the road (like a big storm or a road race—or a school dance, in my case).

The key takeaway point here is that while opportunists can't always count on opportunities, entrepreneurs *can count on themselves* to create their own opportunities for the future—opportunities that will lead to a successful business.

Even though I've been running Mo's Bows for eight years, I'd still say I'm at the beginning of my entrepreneurial journey. I'm in the game and I'm getting better at it every day, but I still have things to learn and ways in which I can improve to build an even better, more successful business. But the fact that since my first sale I've wanted to find a way to do this forever is all the drive I need to make the future of my company quite solid.

Once your business is running smoothly, what would you do if you had to start over to make it even more successful?

The reality of business is that you *sell your business every night* when you go to bed, and *you buy it back* first thing in the morning. A lot of people go out of business because they don't adapt to changes in the market or customers. Maybe you have a lawn-mowing business but the price of gas becomes so high that you can't offer the same rates you used to, and then you start losing customers due to your escalating rates. How will you keep running a successful business under the current conditions?

Here's my big tip: Stop worrying about the future (I'm serious). It will get here soon enough. Think of the apps and games you have on your phone. Some of them improve over time and add features. But these apps will improve and get better only with the help and feedback of customers who enjoy these apps. Remember, not all "products" are physical. If you have a lawn-mowing business, you can offer a special package in the fall that includes raking leaves. That might help to stabilize or increase your business during a difficult time. Adding fresh products to your lineup can help you with some of your business's biggest problems, too. Video game companies and apps constantly add new levels and services to keep users engaged with their products.

Below are a few tips I've learned to help your business adapt and to keep you in a growth mind-set:

1. Don't worry about the competition. Instead, become the competition by anticipating the newest trends, what your customer may want next, and what the next biggest thing is in your industry.

2. Avoid stagnation by building new products while continuing to offer your original goods or services. Just as learning to make bow ties helped me learn how to sew, adding neckties and other products recently has helped me learn new skills that will help my company as it expands into making clothes. This will help you try out new methods and learn new skills. Karen should always look for new ways to offer products so she can stay in business year-round, even when lawn mowing isn't at its peak, and Dave should find new flavors to sell at his lemonade stand just to keep his existing customers coming by frequently and to expand to new customers who want lemonade with a special flavor.

3. Don't do what everyone else is doing. Think outside the box. But more than that, create your own box where there are new ideas and innovative ways to change the world and to drive business or interest in what it is you are doing.

✤ ✤ ✤

Just a few short months after Mo's Bows reached that plateau of "just good enough," I got a call from the sports network ESPN. They'd seen me on TV and wanted me to go out and work the red carpet for the NBA Draft in 2015. They told me that I could use that platform to talk about the cool outfits all the young ballplayers wore to the event.

Thinking with my entrepreneur brain, I knew this opportunity would help me make some incredible connections and help keep Mo's Bows from stagnating. Just getting an invitation alone was worth it for me to attend the event.

However, I thought back to my zero-dollar marketing knowledge and figured that I could use that to my advantage in this case. As a *tastemaker*, I was in a unique situation. I would try to help Mo's Bows go viral using this event as a platform. All I needed to do was to give the *communities* of viewers and influencers something memorable to discuss. And I needed that *surprise* factor.

So I showed up at the event with a handmade bow tie for all of the future NBA Draft picks. Needless to say, this foresight on my part, along with strong mentoring from Daymond, allowed me to take Mo's Bows to a whole new level. I had made it beyond the "just good enough" hurdle.

The following year, I signed an official licensing deal with the NBA to sell Mo's Bows with basketball team logos on them. This involved significant challenges for my young company. Even now I still tweak my bow tie pattern to improve it, but with this licensing deal, I could also make full-size neckties for NBA fans and players. These were not only our biggest ties (literally, these ties had to be tall enough for LeBron!), but this became my biggest opportunity to rise to the occasion and make Mo's Bows even more of a success.

The lessons I learned that got me to this great opportunity all came out of that first farmers' market experience. And what will help you propel your business from the farmers' market to the NBA is already inside you—you just have to make the opportunities happen for yourself.

Wherever you want to get to in business, you will only get there if you start today. Wanna know how? You should know this by now, so let's repeat together:

BELIEVE in yourself!

Look for OPPORTUNITIES.

WORK HARD!

SEEK SUPPORT from friends and family.

Remember: the BOWS of Business are always there to guide you along the way.

14

PARTNERSHIPS

Wow. Look at where you are now!

Take a moment and think about your business. Are you outshining your competition? Have you gotten your business into its own category? Even if you haven't achieved these things at this moment, you are well on your way to doing so. And I have to admit, I'm a little bit envious of you. I didn't have any solid blueprints to follow when I started my company, but I hope you feel like you do with all the measuring and cutting you've been learning and applying to your entrepreneurial activities.

Next, I'm going to share with you the secret to increasing your business tenfold. It goes something like this: establish partnerships.

What I mean by this is that if you have early success in your business, you can try to double that success by bringing on a partner who can help you do an equal amount of work.

Think about a time at school when you had to work on a project with a partner. Sometimes you get matched up with a partner who doesn't want to do any work. Or you get a partner who won't let you do any of the work because they think that the way they do things is better. This is not a partnership; it's just two people trying to work together. And this doesn't necessarily mean your project will be a success.

Finding a good partner works a lot like tackling a two-player video game. For example, you and your best friend come home from school and decide to try to beat the first level in a new, challenging video game. Just like in a video game, in business you are *always trying to get to the next level*. Sometimes you work and work and work at the same task on the first level and have mixed success. Even playing with a partner doesn't guarantee that you'll get to the next level any faster. Sometimes even having *ten* partners helping you out won't get you to the next level any faster.

Everybody needs partners when there is a lot of work to be done. You and your partner are interchangeable. But now think of the example of a lemonade stand. If you and your partner both sit at the stand all day, you'll not only need a larger table and two chairs but also have to sell double the lemonade to split the profits equally and still have enough to put back into your business. Having you and your partner tackle the same tasks doesn't really make sense from a business standpoint. Ideally, you would want your partner to do one task (maybe taking the customers' money), while you do another task to make your business more efficient (you pour the glass of lemonade for your customer). Learning to work with other people is an important part of business, so finding a partner you can work with is key.

In business, however, there is a difference between finding *partners* and finding *partnerships*. I recommend you look for *partnerships* over *partners*. And here's why.

Not only is a *partnership* next-level business, but it will also take your business *to the next level.* At the early stages of my bow tie business, I physically sold every single bow tie I made. That meant I did person-to-person sales for each bow tie that was ordered. This took not only a *lot* of sales to make my business profitable, but a lot of effort as well. Sometimes I had to have my mom drive me across town to deliver just one bow tie—that's not so efficient with the cost of gas. Through this early process, I learned a lot and ultimately decided that this wasn't the most cost-effective way to run a business, after all.

Even though I was hand-selling my bow ties at the very beginning, I did quickly have a lot of partners working with me to help me get off the ground. First, I had just Granny and Mom, and then slowly I added a couple of family members to take on additional workflow. Making high-quality bow ties takes time. And bow ties aren't like lemonade. I had to go and find quality and very expensive fabric and measure out enough for a bow tie without wasting any materials. Then I had to sew each one for each customer. The work took so much time that I could never imagine doing it even ten times in one day just by myself.

But if I entered a partnership that could bring me ten new customers—or just a company that would order ten bow ties for themselves and take on the risk of selling them to *their* customers—I could then decrease the amount of work required to make the ten ties. What I mean by this is that with an order of ten ties up front, I could factor that into one trip to the fabric store, one day of cutting out all ten patterns, one day of sewing the ties, and one day of delivering them, instead of doing each of those steps on ten different days.

There are so many great reasons to look for opportunities to work with other businesses and people. There is an upscale family-owned clothing store in Memphis called Oak Hall. The store has been around since 1859 and has some great history with the city. It is also one of my favorite stores because they carry all of the top brands in men's fashion, including Mo's Bows. Not only do they have great clothes, but the store also has a great reputation. When I agreed to sell my ties in this store, I knew it would be a great partnership. This was a company that not only appreciated the quality of my work but also believed in me and my brand. I appeared on the cover of their magazine, *4Memphis*, and they even featured me on my very first billboard to advertise my bow ties. By being on the billboard and in the magazine, my name, face, and product were introduced to a bigger audience than I would have been able to reach on my own.

When you look to partner with a company, you want to look for someone who shares the same goals and ideas that you have for yourself and your brand. My friends at Oak Hall believe in local businesses, they believe in quality products, and they know the importance of family. We have done great business together over the years, and I'm excited to build my brand with them as a top retailer of my products.

Partnerships can also be as simple as a good working relationship with different organizations. One day in 2013 I received a custom order for fifteen purple-and-gold bow ties from an organization called Jack and Jill of America, Inc. I didn't know much about this organization at the time, so I Googled them. Once I learned more, I realized I needed to have a good working relationship with them. Jack and Jill of America, Inc. is an organization of moms who want to encourage and inspire their

children to focus on things like community, education, and entrepreneurship. These were all of the things my own mom taught me the importance of. Jack and Jill of America, Inc. has more than forty thousand members, with 230 chapters around the world. I've managed to build a relationship with them over the years by speaking at several of their conferences and meetings in Florida, New Jersey, and Tennessee. By working with them, I get to share my story and encourage hundreds of kids to tap into their passions; plus, I always sell a lot of bow ties in the meantime. In fact, out of all of my years of selling bow ties, the only time I've ever *sold out* of all of my bow ties was with a group of Jack and Jill of America, Inc. members.

A good partner is vital for your "viral" success. Your ideal partner is a *tastemaker* and a member of an important *community*. In fact, if you're young and they want to work with you, that might be just the kind of *surprise* that will hook people into checking out what you do.

❖ ❖ ❖

But a true partnership is *mutually beneficial.* Whether it's a TV show, an organization like the Boys and Girls Club, or even my first retail partners: The people I wanted to partner with also saw a value in partnering with me. They didn't do it just to be friendly.

I remember walking into a men's clothing store for the first time. The store was covered in gray carpet, and everyone who worked and shopped there seemed to be a lot older. Usually, I would go to this store after school when it was mostly empty. That should tell you everything you need to know about partnerships right there. I came into this store looking for new customers. And what did this store need more than anything? *New customers.*

I could have used this as an opportunity to ask the store if I could sell my bow ties along with their existing ties. But I was thinking like an entrepreneur, and instead I sold the store manager a story of how to increase their customer base. I told the manager that at my school, the third graders participated in what was called "Bow Tie Wednesday" but that no one in our town sold cool bow ties.

Once I had the manager's interest, that's when I sold him what *I* could bring to *his* store for both of us to capitalize on this hole in the market. I effectively sold him a new breed of customer and offered him a lot more than just that. I promised that if he wanted to sell my bow ties in his store, I would leverage my social media (which was growing stronger by the week) to bring in new customers to his store.

Take a step back and look at this scenario from the store's perspective: If kids as young as ten and eleven came into their men's clothing store and saw that the store cared about what they wanted (in this case, bow ties), what might happen next? Those young customers might be likely to buy a bow tie or two, and then, as they got older, they might decide to return to the store to buy a suit for their first high school dance or for when they graduate from college because they will have had a good experience with the store from a very early age by seeing that they carried a product they were seeking.

Ultimately, when I visited men's clothing stores and told the owners my story, I didn't just sell them bow ties; I sold them a new type of customer altogether.

This is what I mean by making a true partnership. In the case of Mo's Bows, instead of being a scrappy company started from scraps of fabric, now it's the youngest brand to be featured in the best clothing stores in town. Look at my social media. Now instead of a picture of a nice bow tie, you've got a picture of me with a big smile on my face shaking hands with the owner of the store with hundreds of my ties on the table.

I love to tell this story, because it shows that anyone—even a kid—can start a business and take it to the next level. You, too, have what it takes. You just need to believe in yourself and get creative in thinking about how you can build partnerships within your industry.

So, who do you know who can get you to the next level in your business? Who would be willing to take a chance on you? Hint: it's probably somebody who needs you as much as you need them.

Think about finding a partnership where that company or person has a social media following that counts on them for great stories about what's going on in their industry and community. Maybe they have already overcome the biggest issues you're facing and can help you tackle those obstacles (more on that in the next chapter).

Partnerships will often introduce you to great mentors as well. One thing I learned from a mentor I had is this: You are the average of the five people you spend the most time with. So the best way to level up in your business game is by forming a great partnership.

THE END OF
PART 2

By now, you have the tools and even the supplies to get your business off the ground. Maybe you unconsciously know that you have a limited supply of opportunities and even *supplies*, so perhaps you are avoiding diving into the hard stuff. That's what this part, "Cut," has been all about.

This part of setting up a business can be scary. You might burn through all of your supplies and support on your first project. But as an entrepreneur, you will pursue opportunity *regardless of the resources controlled*. For that reason, it's important to measure those resources and then cut them down to see what you can do successfully. For most young entrepreneurs, this won't be the last empire ever started, but everything you do going forward will have benefited from the work you do now on your first business venture.

Making cuts can be messy—whether in fashion, lemonade sales, or even life. But just like my granny did, you can save the scraps from those early attempts and come back to them later. Maybe they'll come in handy, or maybe you can pass them on to others as you focus on a new idea or venture. Remember that those scraps may look like a waste to some, but to your grandkids they could look like the beginning of a bright and successful business future.

STITCH

In the "Measure" part of this book, you learned about many places to find resources you didn't know you had. In "Cut," you got the tools you need to become bold enough to figure out what your product is made of. And now you are about to embark on the most important part, "Stitch," which is all about putting everything together to create the most successful business you can.

After I appeared on *Shark Tank*, people began approaching me, saying things like, "Now you've really got your work cut out for you." I found this to be a funny statement for them to make.

What is typically meant by this common phrase is that 99 percent of the work a fashion designer does is in designing, sourcing, and measuring out the pieces of project and the person who puts all these pieces together has it easy. I'm here to tell you that, yes, 99 percent of the work is done by the time you get to actually stitching together your product. But 99 percent of your product depends on how well you put it all together in that last 1 percent of the job.

I will discuss some of the most common problems you will face as you try to stitch all the parts of your business together in order to get it up and running successfully. You can *measure* your product perfectly; you can *cut* it out perfectly. But how you *stitch* it all together will take most of your entrepreneurial muscle to make a successful business.

15

STITCH IT TOGETHER AND TIGHTEN IT UP

The hardest part of starting your own business, I believe, is learning how to *keep* your business going. It's hard because you as a young entrepreneur are faced with balancing your time between school, friends, and keeping your business fresh and up-to-date. It becomes hard to stay focused on all of those tasks. By now making money might even come *too* easily for you since you've found your groove. Or you may have been spending most of your time tackling problems or dealing with business surprises that creep up out of nowhere that prevent you from moving your business forward. Or worse, you may have come so far and find an obstacle that you can't overcome on your own now.

The casual businessperson will make it this far and give up. But remember that *"entrepreneurship is the pursuit of opportunity without regard to resources currently controlled."* A lot of the people you think of as entrepreneurs are really just opportunists, as I've discussed earlier in this book. The opportunists see an opening one time, take their "business" as far as it can go, and then abandon it when the opportunity disappears. Some, though not all, will take that opportunity and go into another business, but it's not for everyone.

You already have all the tools you need to "stitch" your business together and make it stick. Just remember the BOWS of Business. Below is a scenario that we can work out together using the tools you've learned so far. (Whenever you get stuck, return to the BOWS of Business. And whenever you want to accelerate your business and bring it to the next level, you must remember to Measure—Cut—Stitch.)

You have run a successful lemonade stand all summer, and now winter is coming. Not only will you not have the same summer foot traffic, but the kids in school have started to see your success and are copying your business model. You know that by spring, you will have more competition and make potentially less money. So what should you do?

In the scenario above, you had a good year, but you have a hard year ahead of you. That's okay! You don't want to run a lemonade stand for the rest of your life, right? So first:

BELIEVE in yourself! You made it this far all on your own. You had to figure out each step along the way. Anyone who copies you will benefit from that, so you will just have to stay two steps ahead the next time around. Staying two steps ahead might mean creating new flavors or looking for a different way to sweeten your lemonade. Also, a new paint color on your stand might give a fresh look to your company.

Look for OPPORTUNITIES to give back. Maybe at the end of the year you have some sugar or lemons that will expire by spring. Why not make a nice big batch of lemonade and give it away to your school, church, or community members as a way of saying thanks for a great year? This is a wonderful way to surprise and delight your customers. Just think: by donating lemonade to different organizations, they may consider you for future events where you can sell your lemonade and meet more customers. Show potential customers and partners why other people would like *your* product over the competition. People will remember the generous gesture come next spring, I promise.

WORK HARD! Even when you give your product away for free, you are still building your customer base and growing your social media. Whether you are donating or selling your product, it's always a good idea to collect emails or contact information from customers. I carry a piece of paper with me at all events so I can be sure to stay in touch with everyone who shows an interest in my company and product. Putting in the work also means looking for ways to innovate your lemonade. Maybe it's time for different cups and packaging. Take some time to sit and brainstorm on ways to innovate.

Look for SUPPORT from family and friends! Maybe you have already pitched and sold your product to everyone you know. But what about your family? Whether you're selling lemonade or bow ties, you will always benefit from learning about a new customer base by asking those who are closest to you for their help and guidance.

You've learned a lot about how to plan for success up to this point. But how do you plan for "just okay"? It's easily one of the hardest parts of being an entrepreneur. Maybe you've gotten into business because you see how easily the world could be better by something you can bring to it. But then with a little success under your belt, you soon notice why it's so easy just to coast along.

So much of your early success in your business depends on the luck you find. But what happens when that luck runs out? If you quit now just because your opportunities run out, are you really an entrepreneur, or are you just an opportunist?

You decide.

Everything that got you to where you are—whether you are just starting out, you have some setbacks, or your success has brought you a whole new set of problems—came from inside you. The solution will come from inside you, too.

Now you gotta get into that production rhythm: Measure, Cut, Stitch. Measure your business, cut what doesn't bring you positive results, and stitch it back together. If nothing seems to be working, rip it up and start again by using everything you've learned so far!

Seasoned entrepreneurs will tell you: 99 percent of your work to build a successful business will come at the last 1 percent of the project. Knowing that, are you too afraid to get started in the first place? Or will you dive in knowing that you have all the time in the world to find a successful path forward?

The best advice I can give you is simply to trust yourself. You made it 99 percent of the way. And everything you learned to get there will apply to that last 1 percent of the journey. When you have your "work cut out for you," you won't be able to switch off your entrepreneur mode—I'm sure of it.

If today I handed you a stack of precut bow ties, you might stitch them together right away. But after two or three ties, you might come up with a better way to stitch. By the time you finish making ten ties, you might think of a better way you could have made them faster from the beginning. The key in business is to always move forward and to be an entrepreneur of your talents. After ten ties are done, you might think, for example, of how you could cut them better if you could start over today. When I first started cutting out bow ties, I cut them one at a time. But I later learned from my seamstress Sherry Miller that you can stack the fabric and use a special blade to cut several ties at once.

As an entrepreneur, you owe it to everyone you work with to work better every time. Measure better, cut better, and stitch better.

Be better!

Let your greatness be contagious. Now with your spirits up, you can start planning your next move. Remember: You started your business because you love doing it. Try to always have some fun with it!

16

MANAGING
THE MONEY

F irst, let's define what money really is for the entrepreneur especially. For many kids, money is a scarce resource that keeps them from pursuing their dreams. But since kids can be entrepreneurs, they have learned *"the pursuit of opportunity without regard to resources currently controlled."* Can money be the resource in question here?

For most young entrepreneurs, the business game is all about getting a small amount of money so you can buy the resources you need. Maybe your parents cut you a deal and say you can have a new phone or a new bike if you pay for half of it. So you dig in, you get a book about how to get started in business (like this one), and you make enough money to hold up your end of the deal.

But what if you could make enough money to simply buy the things you really want without having to even split the costs with your parents? Money helps with running your company and provides you the ability to expand and grow. The smartest thing to do is to save and invest the money you make, although it may be a little tricky, especially at first. But if you save now, then you will be prepared for many rainy days ahead.

If you've never had more than a couple of bucks in your pocket, the first time you actually *do* make some money, you may find yourself spending it super quickly. And that's okay. You earned the money, so you can decide what to do with it. But what if I told you that instead of working for your money, you could make your money work for you? Confusing? I'll explain more below.

Let's plan out what a small business will spend and earn in a week. To do this we need to know a few things:

1. **Keep track of your expenses.** In a notebook or on a computer spreadsheet, write down how much you spent, when you spent it, where you spent it, and what you bought. Keeping your receipts for any purchases will help you better create this spreadsheet.

2. **Know your numbers.** How much have you sold or earned today? This week? Since you first started your business? Remember: **revenue** minus **expenses** equals **profit**. There will be an example of how this works below.

3. **Set up a bank account.** It's a really fun day when you and your parents can go to the bank to set up an account just for you! The money in there will stay put and will be solely yours. You can even keep an eye on it online if your bank has a website. But as an entrepreneur, you should also set up a separate account for your business, especially once you start turning a profit.

Here's an example of the money you will spend and earn in a given week as a business owner. Your revenue is the money people pay you. Your expenses are the money it costs to make that money. You subtract your expenses from your income to determine your profit.

REVENUE		EXPENSES		PROFIT
Farmers' market	$50	Fabric	$15	
Website	$75	Hardware	$15	
Store 1	$100	Product cards	$20	
Store 2	$150	Bags	$20	
Total	$375	Total	$70	$305

So from glancing at this chart, an entrepreneur will be able to tell you that your total revenue was $375, your expenses were $70, and you had a profit of $305.

Simply put: It cost you $70 to earn $305. Not a bad week! That's more than you could make if you got a job after school and earned $10 an hour working six hours every day.

When you keep your expenses on a sheet (such as the one above), you can immediately tell both the health of your company and where you could be saving money. Maybe next week just by spending $2 less on fabric and then cutting $1 each from hardware and product cards, you can save money. If there is a sale on bags, you might not have to buy any the following week. So your next week may look like this:

REVENUE		EXPENSES		PROFIT
Farmers' market	$50	Fabric	$13	
Website	$75	Hardware	$14	
Store 1	$100	Product cards	$19	
Store 2	$150	Bags	$0	
Total	$375	Total	$46	$329

Just by thinking smartly about the way you run your business, you earned $329 in profit the next week. That is a difference of $24 and adds up to $1,248 over a year. That's over $100 per month just from working smarter.

Now think about this: If you use that money to bring in new stores and business, you can reinvest the $100 you save and earn even more money. If you can spend $46 to earn $329 in a week, you can take that $100 per month you saved and invest $46 one week to earn $329 and $46 another week in that month to do it again. Then it would cost you $92 to bring in $658 *extra* in revenue every month. That's $7,896 in *extra revenue* every year.

If some of this seems overwhelming right now, just go ahead and come back to this chapter later on in your journey as an entrepreneur. Every entrepreneur will get great at finding ways to improve their business money-wise. You can do this, too!

As always, it's important to remember the BOWS of Business when it comes to managing money:

BELIEVE in yourself. If you can start a business at your age, you can make it a success just by being smart about your money.

OPPORTUNITIES to give back will help you clear your head when you feel like you've been staring at spreadsheets all day. Do a product giveaway on Instagram or donate your services to a local library fund-raiser, and don't worry about the money you lost on doing something for free. People will remember you and likely purchase your product down the road.

WORK HARD! Once you see how you can earn an extra $2,000 or $3,000 a year just by keeping an eye on your expenses, there will be no detail that slips by you.

SUPPORT from friends and family is key when learning to manage your money. This is where your parents can really help. Being a parent is like being the CEO of a family. Parents make budgets, and they do cost-cutting measures all the time. Ask your parents to help you figure out your expenses as you start your business. Trust me: they'll be so impressed that you would think like that, they'll likely want to help you in any way they can in order for your business to succeed.

17

BEING AN ENTREPRENEUR EVERY DAY

Five years after starting Mo's Bows and focusing my life on fashion, disaster struck for me and my business. I was accepted into a new charter school, which could have been great for expanding my clientele if it weren't for one small problem: the school's uniform policy.

In my old school, students could wear whatever they wanted. Some kids wore gym clothes to school. I wore my bow ties. As my business goals changed, so did my focus. Now, I started setting my sights on fashion school. I needed to study hard to get into Parsons School of Design in New York City—my ultimate dream. To get the best education where I lived, though, I would have to go to the best school. And that meant attending a new charter school that made me wear a hideous uniform: loose-fitting shirt, cardigan, black socks, and—worst of all—a fat, ugly necktie. Everything about the tie was wrong, from the color to the size of it. It was twice as wide as any kid could ever need. It made me look like I was wearing a bib under my cardigan.

I know. There are worse things in life than having to wear a terrible school uniform. But at the time it made me feel like I'd taken a huge step back. I had started my business because I liked how I felt when I looked good, and I wanted to share that feeling with kids everywhere, as well as give adults the permission to feel young again in great accessories. I spent years in the best clothing stores, getting advice from the biggest names in fashion on how to make my business a success.

For the first few weeks at my new school, I would come home almost every day in a bad mood. I couldn't wait to get out of that uniform and into my own clothes. It must have looked funny when the neighbors saw me run inside in my gray school uniform and then run back outside minutes later in fun socks, a stylish jacket, one of my bow ties, and a big smile on my face.

At first I thought that I was helpless to do anything about the school uniform that I hated wearing. But then I remembered that *entrepreneurship is the pursuit of opportunity without regard to resources currently controlled.* I could definitely figure out something to help me feel better wearing a school uniform by staying true to myself and my growing brand.

To some people, there might only be a very small difference between my bow tie and jacket and the school's uniform—let's say it's only 4 percent different. But entrepreneurs know that a final percent makes *all* the difference. Even though I only had to make my uniform 4 percent better, I just couldn't do it; I felt paralyzed. After years of helping people look good and feel good in my bow ties, I'd started to see my new school necktie as a mark of shame. What was all this work for if Mo couldn't even wear Mo's Bows?

What was I doing wrong?

As it turned out, I had forgotten all about the things I have been teaching you in this book. I needed to Measure, Cut, Stitch my own life back together. Sure, I could pinch the extralong part of my school necktie and show my mom where it went wrong. But I failed to do anything about it. When you point out where something else has gone wrong, you're really just doing Part 1: "Measure."

To fix that you need to have the guts to make cuts.

But making cuts works only if you can stitch it back together. I was in a new school, and I didn't want to get into trouble. If I got kicked out, I might lose my chance of getting into Parsons for fashion school.

As an entrepreneur, you need to learn to talk to yourself like a mentor. Like *you're* your biggest fan. What would you say to young Mo, who was just starting a new school, when he started to get down on himself? What would *you* do if you came to a problem like the hideous school uniform—a problem where you didn't have control over the resources?

You'd say the following to young Mo:

BELIEVE in yourself! You've sewn thousands of bow ties. Are you going to be afraid of resizing one necktie and possibly being reprimanded for it?

Think of your OPPORTUNITIES to give back! You don't know many kids at this new school. But maybe if you learned to fix your tie, you could fix ties for others, too.

WORK HARD! Neckties are more complex than bow ties. But that doesn't make them impossible to make.

from friends and family. Ask them what they think of a new necktie or see if they can help you in altering the current tie you already have.

Thanks for your pep talk to young Mo. Here's what happened:

One night during my freshman year of high school, I came home and talked to my mom. I told her that I knew this school was best for me, but that I was feeling drained by the uniform. How was I supposed to focus on fashion when I was so uncomfortable all day in the clothes I was wearing? I understand the concept of a uniform, but, geez, did I have to look exactly like the other 150 boys at my school? My mom stayed up late with me that night, and we took the seam ripper to my school necktie. I decided to change the big, oversized necktie to a skinny necktie. The skinny necktie along with my custom tailored pants would give my uniform a modern and vintage look just for me. It was so cool to tear that necktie apart and see how other companies made ties. The school uniform code only said that the tie had to be the school colors. And when we tore it up, we found a heavier interfacing layer on the inside that made the tie too puffy. We tore that layer out, cut the extra fabric, and created a new skinny necktie—and it felt so good.

My mom was there to support me that night, and together we made a Mo's Bows skinny necktie out of my school uniform's tie, just like the first few times we made bow ties together. From the scraps of the old tie, we made something just for me. When I went to school wearing my skinny necktie, I was sort of expecting my teacher to mention the uniform dress code, but he didn't. There was a lot of talk about the tie, but from other students. I was actually surprised that some upperclassmen wanted to know where I bought the tie and wanted me to make some for them. As a freshman in high school, that was a great icebreaker for me, and I became friends with juniors and seniors within the first week of school.

❖ ❖ ❖

This experience actually led me to decide to start making more neckties. Sure, everyone knew me for my bow ties. But all that work and the great story I'd been telling all along really helped me to branch out. And guess what? A lot of people who would never buy a bow tie were more than happy to purchase one of my neckties instead. One thing I learned early when I started my business was how important it is to be true to myself. That means being comfortable with me. It's important to recognize who you are, whether an athlete, a chef, or a designer, and stay true to yourself.

18

WORTH MORE
THAN MONEY

We've spent so much of this book getting you in the right mind-set to start your business. It takes so much energy and commitment to get it off the ground. But now I want to help you set your sights higher. I've told you how you can improve your life, but can you improve your life even more just by helping others out?

When summer hits Memphis, I can barely stand outside. Getting out of a car in the middle of the day is challenging enough, as the metal on the car door handle can actually burn you! Even if you go to a swimming pool, you might burn your feet just walking across the hot pavement around the pool before you dive in. The best way to escape the heat of a Memphis summer is to get out of the city. And if you are a kid, that means attending summer camp.

Now, they don't really teach about entrepreneurship in school, but in a way they do so at summer camp. At the camp I used to attend, my fellow campers and I would play games, go on different field trips, and, of course, go swimming. We would learn different art skills and meet new friends. Even though this was only a day camp, they also provided kids with breakfast and lunch. It was so much better than staying at home or playing in the street.

I always enjoyed my summers mainly because I attended summer camp. I remember once, when I was nine years old, my mom was driving me to camp one morning and I saw a bunch of kids playing on the hot city streets. I asked her why those kids didn't also go to camp instead of staying home all summer. She told me that some kids can't afford to go to camp (in fact, when I was really young, she said she didn't have enough money to send me to camp, either).

That got me thinking about how to help kids escape the heat of the city in the summers. As Mo's Bows grew more and more successful and I earned more and more profits, I decided that every year I'd pick one special tie and then give all the profits of sales of that particular tie to the Go Mo Scholarship fund (I set this up in 2012). My hope is that when customers can't make an easy choice between tie colors, they may be more likely to choose the tie that will benefit other children and help them have a better life.

The only differences between me and other children are the opportunities I've found and created. But even if I could have learned that in a book, I learned how much I loved being creative at summer camp. I want to give other kids the opportunity to learn and discover something amazing.

Since setting up the Go Mo Scholarship, I've been able to send more than fifty kids to summer camp by selling my special

Go Mo Bow Tie. Some of the kids I've helped come from places where they can't always count on having a good meal or good activities. In fact, childhood hunger is at its highest in the summer months. But by setting up this scholarship, I can help at least a few of them have a fun summer full of outdoor activities and solid meals.

Now whenever I wonder if running my business is worth it, I just think of all the kids I have been able to help. My success is their success. It's like having someone to celebrate good news with. Being an entrepreneur isn't about being straitlaced and businesslike all the time. It's about taking your sense of childlike wonder and applying it to your own future.

Maybe those kids I help send to camp will learn new skills from each other. Maybe they will start a business together. But most important, every day they will get an opportunity that they can never get back as they get older. They get to be kids again.

All of the tips, tricks, and advice in this book came from what I learned while stitching together several thousand bow ties over the past eight years.

Since I began writing this book, my life and the life of my company have immensely changed. I'm traveling around the world sharing my story and encouraging other kids to tap into their passion and dream big now. I continue to create bow ties for both children and adults and have included adult neckties and pocket squares in my various collections. Currently, I'm manufacturing my product here in Tennessee just two hours outside my hometown of Memphis. Having my bow ties handmade in the

USA has always been very important to me, and it allows me to visit with the seamstresses and work closely with them to make my creative ideas come to life. My mom and I have started the Mo's Bows Foundation as a resource for youth and family entrepreneurship. Now I get to share my experiences and mentor other young entrepreneurs. My next goal as a young entrepreneur is to start my own clothing line. And guess where that puts me? Right back at step 1: measure. And, from there, I will then have to cut and stitch and maybe repeat it all again before I get that business in the same successful spot Mo's Bows is currently in.

I know I will encounter some problems setting up a new business, as well as have my fair share of self-doubt along the way. I will get frustrated and wonder why I chose to go into the fashion business in the first place. But when I get into a corner, I will now have *you* to remind me to think back on the BOWS of Business: to BELIEVE in myself, to look for OPPORTUNITIES to give back, to WORK HARD, and to look for SUPPORT from my friends and family. And if I do that, I'm sure—just like you— to make a successful business venture no matter where life takes me.

Please join the Mo's Bows community on Facebook, Instagram, and Twitter and feel emboldened to share your dreams with the rest of the young entrepreneurs out there. Remember: It's not the opportunities you have in life, it's what you make of them. Your first instinct might be to find something you're already good at so that you will havemore success doing what comes easily. But that's not what Measure, Cut, and Stitch is all about.

Don't go out into the world hoping for an easy business life. Measure, cut, and stitch together the future that you want for

yourself. It's not something that will just happen; you have to *make* it happen. It's not a magic spell or a winning lottery ticket. Being an entrepreneur means starting with nothing and working to create what you want to see in the world—and in yourself as a businessperson. You must never be afraid to start over, either, because that's all part of the road toward success. Simply keep in mind that you started from nothing once and you are a better entrepreneur now than you were then. Do not hope for tasks equal to your skills; instead, pray for skills that are equal to your tasks. Then the future tasks will be easier for you to handle, not because they were easy but because they match your skill set.

I promise you that once you start making your own money, you will never want to work for someone else. You will know on the inside that no one can hurt you, no one can stand in your way, and no dream is too crazy to chase.

Plus, all you make is *your* money. If you really do save $30,000 and you want to spend some time traveling the world after high school or college, or if you want to set out and invest in your own business, no one can stop you because you've done what is necessary to make this a reality.

The important thing about being an entrepreneur is to just let yourself be you. Dream big. Be big. Learn how to work out the details. Remember: the difference between you and any other person is all in the details.

Now comes the part that no one else will tell you: how proud of yourself you should be. I'm proud of you for being brave enough to think boldly with me. You're young, you're smart, and you're already way ahead of others on your journey. Any decision you make going forward is a decision you've figured out on your own instead of a choice that someone forced you to make.

I told you in the very beginning that I wish this book had been around when I started out in business. Now that you've read it, you are ready to get out there and be great in whatever entrepreneurial adventure you take. There is nothing more humbling than starting your own business, so remember to BELIEVE in yourself, look for OPPORTUNITIES to give back, WORK HARD, and SEEK SUPPORT from friends and family whenever the going gets a little tough. And, most important, have a lot of fun.

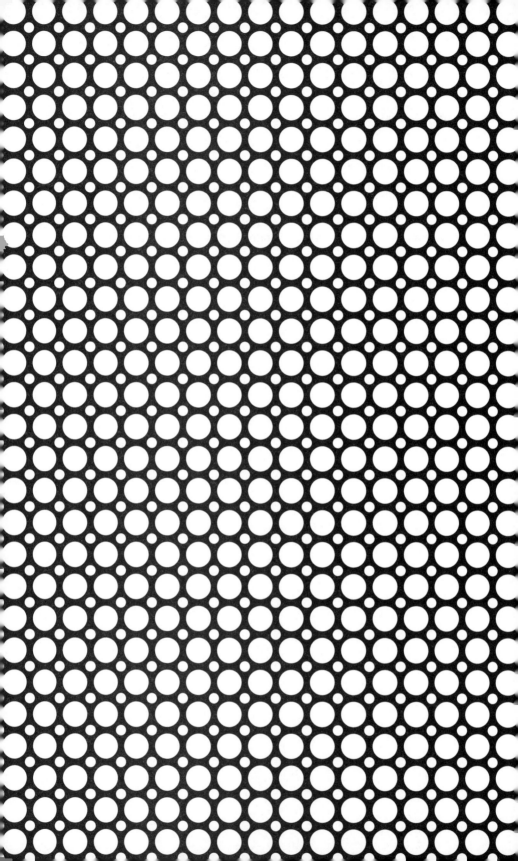

THE ENTREPRENEUR'S GLOSSARY: LEARN THE LINGO

Every business has its own jargon, or slang, for the words and tools that keep the business humming. Next time you watch a movie, stay until the very end and when the credits roll, you'll see all the funny job titles of the people who have worked on the movie. For example, there's usually a key grip, a gaffer, and a best boy. What does the key grip do? Set up the lights. What does the gaffer do? Helps the key grip. What does the best boy do? Runs a different kind of light.

If you went on a TV or movie set today, you might just say, "Why don't you call them all 'the lighting people'?" Well, they have specific job titles because, for example, the best boy needs to talk to the gaffer, and the director needs to know which one can do which task. Production on set flows a lot smoother when everyone knows precisely what job they need to do.

Jargon can confuse outsiders, but its real purpose is to reduce confusion among insiders. You and your friends—and people you know at school—might all use slang that people from another school wouldn't get. It's like an inside joke.

Let's say you have a substitute teacher named Mr. Bobkins. When Mr. Bobkins announces that there will be spaghetti at lunch, you might glance at your friend and smile. Now, Mr.

Bobkins doesn't know the story of the time your friend Mike ordered spaghetti for lunch but then tripped on the way to the cafeteria and spilled it all over his shirt. If you had to stop and tell Mr. Bobkins that whole story, you might get in trouble. So, instead, you glance at a friend and smile.

See how that inside joke helped you communicate better and faster with your friend? Jargon works pretty much the same in business.

This book, for example, has a writer, an editor, an agent, and a publisher. They all have different jobs, but they are working toward the same goal: to publish this book and make it available to you, the reader!

So let's get your business jargon, lingo, and collective slang down. That way, whenever you meet another entrepreneur, you will speak the same language right away.

The following are the most important terms in business to know, and I'll use the example of a lemonade stand or a lawn-mowing business or Mo's Bows after the definition of each term to help explain exactly how it is used in an everyday business context.

Angel investor: this is a person who invests in your company early on.

*We had enough money for only one gallon of lemonade, but an **angel investor** came in and helped us get supplies for three more gallons.*

Appraisal: a formal estimate of how much a product or service is worth to someone else.

*It costs one dollar to make a gallon of lemonade, but the average **appraisal** for that gallon is ten dollars.*

Brand: a name, term, or design that distinguishes your product or service from others.

*Three people sold lemonade on our street, but our **brand** of local, organic lemonade stood out as the best.*

Capital: money saved or spent to further your business.

*Our first day of sales left us with enough **capital** to fund three more days' worth of selling.*

Client: the user of your product or service, often used interchangeably with **customer**.

*Our favorite **customer** buys lemonade every Saturday, and now her boss at the local café is a great **client** and orders one gallon from us every week.*

Elevator pitch: a brief, one-sentence description of who you are and what you're selling. It should be short enough to explain it to an outsider in the time it takes to ride the elevator.

Someone complimented my bow tie in the elevator at the mall and I said, "Thank you, I designed it for my company, Mo's Bows. We make high-quality fashion items for kids and adults that you can find here at stores like Neiman Marcus."

Entrepreneur: a person who organizes and operates his or her own **venture**.

*I started a lemonade stand for my first **venture** as an **entrepreneur**, and for my second **venture** I started a lawn-mowing business.*

Marketing: the process of researching, promoting, selling, and distributing your product or service.

Our second lemonade stand doesn't get much foot traffic, so we are doing some **marketing** *to find a more visible location.*

Materials: everything you need to get *before* you can make your product.

Before making our first batch of lemonade, we went to the store for lemons, sugar, and other **materials.**

MVP: minimum viable product—your very first stage of production.

We tried out our first lemonade recipe by making an **MVP** *of lemon-flavored Kool-Aid to see if it would sell on a hot day.*

Outsourcing: purchasing services from another company. Businesses hire other businesses typically for accounting and advertising but also for packaging and materials.

After a week of squeezing our own lemons, we **outsourced** *to a local juice company to save time and energy.*

Packaging: everything you need to get your product into your client's hands for a given amount.

We decided to go with a small yellow cup as **packaging** *for our lemonade stand. Or in another example: Our lawn mower sold a* **"package deal"** *of mowing the lawn and trimming the hedges for a set price.*

Patent: a property right granted to an inventor to exclude others from making, using, or offering for sale any original invention.

After perfecting our lemonade, we applied for a **patent** *to keep people from stealing our recipe.*

Product: the goods or services you offer.

*Whether the customer buy a single glass or gets a gallon of our lemonade delivered, we always offer the finest **product**.*

Product testing: trying out new ways to improve the goods or services you offer

*My friends are starting their own lemonade stand, so we've been **product testing** new recipes all week.*

Public relations (PR): the deliberate promotion of a specific image for a business.

*We sent the local website images of our lemonade stand and gave out samples for free at the street fair as a good use of **public relations**.*

Sales: the exchange of a product or service for money.

*We sell a glass of lemonade for $1, and on a busy day our **sales** can be $200.*

Scale: the ability to increase the size of your business by growing, not just by doing more volume.

*For the Mo's Bows Fall Collection, I usually buy more fabric in order to **scale** up bow tie production before the holiday season.*

Service: a company may be in the business of offering a set amount of work for sale in a **package**.

*We offer complete lawn care as a **service**, and with the money we earn we can **outsource** the work of **PR**, **packaging**, and **marketing** to another company so we can focus on developing new **products** to sell.*

Value: the outcome of an **appraisal**.

*On a hot day, people really **value** a cold glass of lemonade enough that they will pay a dollar for something that costs us ten cents to make.*

Venture: an entrepreneur can operate several different businesses, and each one is called a different *venture*. (I like to think that this is the best part of your entrepreneurial *ad*venture.)

*We used the money from our lemonade stand to start a second **venture** in the lawn-mowing business.*

Venture capital: a form of investment in which the entrepreneur gives up partial ownership of their company in exchange for the money they need to accelerate their business (typically from $500,000 to $5 million).

*Because I **patented** my recipe, we raised $1 million in **venture capital** to start bottling my **brand** of lemonade in exchange for 10 percent of my company.*

Now that you have your "business slang" down, I want you to think of this as another tool to help make your work in starting and growing your business go smoothly.

ACKNOWLEDGMENTS

I want to take this time to thank everyone involved with making my very first book project a reality. I'm thankful to my editor, Julie Matysik, for her vision to publish a book that will no doubt be a great tool for future kidpreneurs and for her clear understanding of the way my teenage brain works. Also, thanks to my book agent, Kirsten Neuhaus, who planted the seed for this book and patiently guided me through the entire process. A very special thank-you to my fellow stylish storyteller Brendan Jay Sullivan for his creative talent and enthusiasm. I would also like to thank all the folks at Shark Branding and my awesome mentor Daymond John for writing a great foreword and for always being there for me no matter what. Thank you to a few good men who have been solid rocks for me and my mom since we started Mo's Bows: Grandpa Steve, Joshua McCain, Khomorai Galloway, Larry Galloway, Michael Wilson, and Eric Robertson. A huge thank-you to Shun Watkins, Shemia Morris, Debra Mobley, and Raven Cheatham for your never-ending love and support.

And last, with everything in me, I thank my mom for believing in me almost more than I believe in myself.

ABOUT THE AUTHORS

MOZIAH "MO" BRIDGES is the seventeen-year-old creative director and founder of Mo's Bows Handmade Bow Ties, a Memphis-based and family-run business.

After trading bow ties for rocks on the school playground, Moziah's strong fashion sense led him to start his own company at the age of nine. With the help of his mother and retired seamstress grandmother, Moziah began selling bow ties on his website (mosbowsmemphis.com) and in Memphis retail stores.

His colorful, handmade ties quickly made an impression on major networks, and the young fashion mogul made rounds on *The Steve Harvey Show, The Today Show, O: The Oprah Magazine, Good Morning America, 20/20, CBS This Morning*, the Disney Channel, and the hit ABC show *Shark Tank*.

In addition to being featured in various international documentaries and publications, the teenage CEO was inducted into the Tennessee State Museum Costume and Textile Institute in 2014 and then took his fashion expertise to a new level in 2015. Moziah not only served as the fashion correspondent for the 2015 NBA Draft but was also twice on *Time*'s list of "30 Most Influential Teens." Moziah was also invited to the inaugural White House Demo Day, where he was able to personally meet President Barack Obama and give him the special "Obama Blue" Mo's Bow. In 2016 Moziah was on *Fortune*'s "18 under 18" list of the country's most innovative and ambitious teens. By 2017 the National Basketball Association sealed a partnership with the young fashion designer to make custom neckties and bow ties for all thirty NBA teams.

Shark Tank's Daymond John serves as Moziah's mentor as he continues to grow his business. Mo's Bows has five employees, including the "CEO of Mo," a.k.a. Mom, Tramica Morris, and Granny, who taught Moziah how to sew. The business-minded teenager, who handpicks every fabric and approves every visual element, has sold more than $600,000 worth of bow ties and men's accessories.

Mo's Bows are sold in retail stores throughout the United States and Germany and have partnered with Cole Haan, Bloomingdale's, the Home Shopping Network, and Neiman Marcus.

In 2012 Moziah started the Go Mo! Summer Camp Scholarship Fund, a charity focused on sending Memphis children to summer camp. To date, the charity efforts of Mo's Bows have sent more than fifty kids to summer camp.

Currently, Moziah is focused on expanding his apparel design skills by entering as an emerging fashion designer in the 2020 Memphis Fashion Week Fashion Show.

A recently licensed driver, with just one year of high school left, Moziah plans to attend college at Parsons School of Design in New York City and have his own clothing line by the time he receives a degree in fashion. In his spare time, you will find Moziah sketching, designing, thrift shopping, and spending time with friends and family.

Tramica Morris is president and cofounder of Mo's Bows Handmade Bow Ties. Morris also manages her son, teen entrepreneur and fashion designer Moziah Bridges. She believes there is a Mo's Bows idea and concept in every household, so in 2018 she launched the nonprofit organization The Mo's Bows Foundation. The foundation's mission is to mentor, encourage, and empower young entrepreneurs. Morris enjoys traveling with family, dancing, bike riding, all things vintage, and community outreach.

INDEX

Corcoran, Barbara, 29, 76
Creativity, 4–5, 146, 148
Cuban, Mark, 29–30
Customer base, 5, 83, 92, 119, 127
Customers
definition of, 155
feedback from, 57, 59, 65, 108
new customers, 26, 33, 70,
96–97, 100–103, 107–109,
115–120, 127
potential customers, 34, 72–73, 76,
91–97, 100–103
"Cut" process, 62–121, 123, 139,
148–150

D

Determination, 5, 26

E

Early adopters, 57. *See also*
Product testing
Elevator pitch, 31–35, 155. *See also*
Pitches
Entrepreneurs
definition of, 155
opportunities for, 9–10, 20–23
perspectives of, 25–27
success of, 3–5, 26–27, 59
Entrepreneurship. *See also* Business
defining, 3, 48, 67, 125–126, 138
encouraging, 116, 118, 145–148
teaching about, 145–148
understanding, 26–27
Expenses, tracking, 131–135

F

Facebook, 84, 92, 148
Failure, fear of, 32, 37–43
Farmers' markets, 37–39, 43, 100,
107, 110, 133–134
Feedback
from customers, 57, 59, 65, 108
from early adopters, 57
from family and friends, 35, 43, 61,
103
Forbes, 5
4Memphis magazine, 116

Four *P*s, 99–103

G

Gates, Bill, 47–48, 50
Global scale, 83
Glossary, 153–158
Go Mo Scholarship, 146–147
Goals, achieving, 9–10, 23, 34–35,
39–43, 60–61, 148–151
Goals, setting, 38–42, 137, 148
Good Morning America, 6
Gray, Farrah, 34

H

Handshakes, 70, 72, 120
Harvey, Steve, 6, 29, 84, 92
Herjavec, Robert, 29
Home Shopping Network, 4

I

Ideas, 3–4, 9–10, 25, 33–34, 42,
108–109
Impressions, 69–72
Income, tracking, 131–135
Instagram, 6, 84–85, 88–89, 134, 148
Inventions, 3–4, 56, 156
Investors, 29–34, 51–53, 67, 94, 154

J

Jack and Jill of America, Inc.,
116, 118
Jay-Z, 15, 16
Jobs, Steve, 77, 89
John, Daymond, 29, 34, 76, 110

L

Location, importance of, 88, 99–103

M

March of Dimes, 89
Marketing. *See also* Social media
tips
definition of, 156
Four *P*s and, 99–103
importance of, 59

Relationships, building, 67–73, 107, 113–120

Resources, 45–53, 64–65, 105, 115, 121, 156

Revenue, 132–134